Paul Peacock has written books on making your own cheese and sausages, as well as a wide range of other titles on cookery and vegetable gardening. An occasional panellist on BBC Radio 4's *Gardeners' Question Time*, he has a gardening column in the *Daily Mirror* as 'Mr. Digwell' and has contributed to countless gardening and cookery magazines.

Also by Paul Peacock

Make Your Own Bacon and Ham
Grow Your Own Vegetables in Pots and Containers
Making Your Own Cheese
Chickens, Ducks and Bees
How to Make Your Own Sausages
Grandma's Ways for Modern Days
Make Your Own Beer and Cider
Storing Your Home-Grown Fruit and Vegetables
The Seasonal Cookbook
Patio Produce
The Urban Hen

THE
FISH
BOOK

How to *choose*,
prepare and *cook*
fresh fish and seafood

Paul Peacock

A How To Book

ROBINSON

ROBINSON

First published in Great Britain in 2017
by Robinson

1 2 3 4 5 6 7 8 9 10

IMPORTANT NOTE
The recommendations in this book
are solely intended as education and
information and should not be taken as
medical advice.

A CIP catalogue record for this book
is available from the British Library.

ISBN: 978-1-47213-920-7

Typeset by Mousemat Design Limited

Printed and bound in Great Britain by
CPI Group (UK) Ltd, Croydon CRO 4YY

Papers used by Robinson are from well-
managed forests and other responsible
sources.

MIX
Paper from
responsible sources
FSC® C104740

Robinson
An imprint of
Little, Brown Book Group
Carmelite House
50 Victoria Embankment
London EC4Y 0DZ

An Hachette UK Company
www.hachette.co.uk

www.littlebrown.co.uk

How To Books are published by
Robinson, an imprint of Little, Brown
Book Group. We welcome proposals
from authors who have first-hand
experience of their subjects.
Please set out the aims of your book,
its target market and its suggested
contents in an email to
Nikki.Read@howtobooks.co.uk.

Contents

WEIGHT	
Metric	Imperial
25g	1oz
50g	2oz
75g	3oz
100g	4oz
150g	5oz
175g	6oz
200g	7oz
225g	8oz
250g	9oz
300g	10oz
350g	12oz
400g	14oz
450g	1lb

OVEN TEMPERATURES	
Celsius	Fahrenheit
110°C	225°F
120°C	250°F
140°C	275°F
150°C	300°F
160°C	325°F
180°C	350°F
190°C	375°F
200°C	400°F
220°C	425°F
230°C	450°F
240°C	475°F

LIQUIDS		
Metric	Imperial	US cup
5ml	1tsp	1tsp
15ml	1tbsp	1tbsp
50ml	2 fl oz	3tbsp
60ml	2½ fl oz	¼ cup
75ml	3 fl oz	⅓ cup
100ml	4 fl oz	scant ½ cup
125ml	4½ fl oz	½ cup
150ml	5 fl oz	⅔ cup
200ml	7 fl oz	scant 1 cup
250ml	9 fl oz	1 cup
300ml	½ pt	1¼ cups
350ml	12fl oz	1⅓ cups
400ml	¾ pt	1¾ cups
500ml	17 fl oz	2 cups
600ml	1 pt	2½ cups

MEASUREMENTS	
Metric	Imperial
5cm	2in
10cm	4in
13cm	5in
15cm	6in
18cm	7in
20cm	8in
25cm	10in
30cm	12in

Introduction

Environmentalists can be so gloomy. I'm sure they are right, of course, but this book begins with the gloomy bit and the rest is pure fishy heaven. I can't help it: when I see a plate of fish, I get a whopping big smile.

Sadly, overfishing fuelled by profit has meant that the saying 'There are plenty more fish in the sea' is no longer true, because there ain't! The seas were once full of fish, but throughout the twentieth century, methods of catching fish in very large numbers – in order to feed the world's growing population – have brought many species near to extinction.

Almost all the world's greatest fish comes from the North Atlantic and the North East Pacific. Most of these coldwater fish are whisked out of the sea, destined for southern Europe and the Far East, and the same goes for shellfish such as scallops, crabs, lobsters, prawns and langoustines. The UK exports much of our domestic catch, but we also import a large amount of tuna, cod, prawns and salmon.

Sustainable fish

The Marine Stewardship Council (MSC) publishes a list of fish that are sustainable: that is, population numbers are currently sufficient to keep the population stable while allowing a reasonable amount of fishing. The names on the list can change over time as endangered species become sustainable once more, or sustainable ones become endangered. Some supermarkets have a printed version of this list, or you can find it online at msc.org.

Fish farming contributes to our supply of fish, helping to reduce pressure on wild populations. In recent years some of the problems associated with fish farming, particularly sea lice that thrive in the overcrowded waters of the fish farms, have been alleviated by using organic methods.

When shopping for fish, particularly in supermarkets, look for the blue MSC label, which will identify fish from sustainable fisheries. Actually, I cannot understand why supermarkets would sell fish that are not on the list, but it does happen.

At the time of writing the sustainable list includes:

Anchovies	Pike-perch (sander or zander)
Clams	Plaice
Cockles	Pollack
Cod	Razor shells
Crab	Sablefish (black cod)
Dogfish (rock salmon, huss)	Saithe (coley)
Flounder	Salmon
Haddock	Sardines
Hake	Scallops
Halibut	Shrimps/prawns
Herring	Smelt
Hoki	Sole
Lobsters	Swordfish
Mackerel	Toothfish (Chilean sea bass)
Mussels	Tuna
Oysters	Whiting

If in doubt, ask the fishmonger, who will be able to put you right – well, most of the time!

Keep it local

Another question to ask, and this is my last environmental hobby horse before we dive into the glorious world of fish, is the origin of the fish you are buying. I would like to illustrate this by visiting a shop I know in Anglesey.

There has been a fishmonger here for many years, a simple shop, sourcing fish from the local fleet. All manner of fish and seafood is sold there and much of it is cooked on the premises. The lady who runs the shop buys the huge, local lobsters – probably the best lobsters in the world – whose journey from quayside to shop can be measured in metres, not miles.

Next to the shop there is a Chinese takeaway with lobster on the menu. They get theirs from a wholesaler in Manchester, who in turn gets them from a processing plant in Hull, who get theirs from Canada.

The lobsters are smaller, inferior in every way to home-fished specimens and, more to the point, they have come a long way in the process.

If you can, buy fish caught as near to you as possible, for flavour, freshness and for the sake of the planet. This is why I have not included recipes for all of the fish on the sustainable list: if they've been shipped in from far away they may be perfectly 'fresh' to eat, but having been frozen for days, or even weeks, they simply won't speak of the sea. Whenever possible, I try to catch my own fish, though I do understand that this is not a viable proposition for everyone.

The driving force behind this book is flavour, aroma, textures, the enjoyment of fish and the appreciation of our seas and rivers. With a little careful shopping and a keen eye to distinguish good fish, we can enjoy the delights of fish and seafood for ever.

CHAPTER 1

How to choose fish at its best

Until around two hundred years ago we were more likely to eat fresh-water fish than sea fish, simply because it was easier get to the plate before it went off. We took so much fish from rivers that the 'rights' to do so were jealously guarded. Poaching was punished harshly – and still is.

Salmon was once one of the commonest fish in our rivers; in some parts of Britain there were laws forbidding employers to feed their servants or apprentices with salmon more than three times a week.

One of the reasons why centres of civilization developed around the coast and on major rivers is their access to a vast larder of fish and seafood. As new technologies were introduced, this began to change. The invention of the steam engine, for example, and the development of the railways, plus the large-scale harvesting and transportation of ice and, later, its mass production, made it possible to bring fresh fish to inland cities within hours of it being caught. The British love affair with fish and chips began in the mid-nineteenth century.

Fish on Friday, for religious reasons, was once the norm, and there are still many people who like to eat fish on Fridays, often without really knowing why. The Catholic Church has always required that people abstain from meat on Fridays (and at one time it wasn't just Fridays, but also Wednesdays, Saturdays and many holy days throughout the year): they often ate fish instead. Fish was not eaten on Sundays or Mondays, and indeed fish sold on a Monday was most likely caught on the previous Friday and consequently was less fresh than fish found on other days. The same is true today.

These days many people buy frozen fish – often covered in batter, breadcrumbs, pastry or sauce – and as a result we are losing the ability to recognise really fresh fish. I feel it is important to learn about the fish you are buying, and to be able to do this you need to see, to smell, to handle the fish and understand its consistency. You can't do this with fish bought in a box and covered in breadcrumbs.

Fishmongers

One of the main criticisms aimed at supermarkets is the resultant demise of independent retailers, such as fishmongers. Every high street used to have a fishmonger, but over the past thirty years many have gone. As well as supplying, gutting/cleaning and filleting a range of seasonal fish, a visit to the fishmonger was educational. You could get to know more about fish and how to cook it, what fish you could substitute in your recipe, plus ask for advice on how not to ruin it in the pan.

But there is a positive side to supermarkets selling fish. They can afford to buy a lot of fish and sell it at a reasonable price, giving you a great range to choose from at most supermarket fish counters. There is at least one supermarket with a dedicated fishmonger in every community. However, be aware, the staff are not always career fishmongers.

Buying fish from a fishmonger, whether it is on your high street, at a market or in the supermarket, is the best way to judge the freshness of fish. If you can, buy whole fish as they enable you to spot the signs of freshness more easily. They also usually work out cheaper than buying prepared fillets. If you don't like to fillet them yourself the fishmonger will do it for you.

What to look out for when buying fresh fish

★ Generally a fish should look as if it's still alive, just not moving!
★ Eyes – should be clear and shiny, not opaque or cloudy.
★ Gills – should be bright pinky-red, moist and bright. Any sticky film means the fish has been hanging around for some time. Don't buy it. I find the gills are the quickest and best way to spot freshness.
★ Skin – should be shiny and wet-looking, almost slimy but not quite.
★ Scales – should be more or less all in place; avoid fish with areas of patchy scales. The scales shouldn't be sticking up, but lying flat, close to the body of the fish.
★ Smell – should smell pleasantly of the sea, not 'fishy', sickly or bitter. Don't be afraid to have a good sniff. Is there a pleasant aroma in the shop? If there are any strong smells, go elsewhere.

★ Touch the fish if you can. It should be cold, almost slimy, and firm. If the flesh is still firm and springs back when you touch it, it means the fish hasn't lost much moisture so it should be good and fresh. If floppy and spongy, pass it by.

★ If you are buying fillets, avoid discoloured or smelly flesh. The flakes should be consistent, intact, not gaping or falling away. If you gently press the flesh, it should feel firm and springy, not soft and spongy.

Until very recently, some fish were sold alive – eels, mostly. You could get your fishmonger to kill them or do the job yourself, but the process is not pleasant – it is hard work killing an eel. Similarly, some freshwater fish were considered muddy, and were kept in pure water for a few days to cleanse them. These would have to be killed just before they were cooked. You may occasionally see this with carp in Chinese restaurants, and in central European restaurants.

Why does fish deteriorate?

There are a number of reasons why fish goes off more quickly than meat. Fish tend to live in cold conditions, often only a few degrees above freezing, and their enzymes are attuned to this. Non-aquatic animals have enzymes that work at much higher temperatures, and when their meat is kept near zero in a fridge, the enzymes almost stop working altogether – but fish enzymes continue their ordinary operation. The combination of enzyme action and oxidation give the unpleasant, strongly 'fishy' smell we associate with being off.

Keeping fish at 0°C, always on ice, makes a marked difference to its keeping properties – even 2°C above this can be detrimental. Vacuum sealing and keeping the fish very cold is even better, but it must be proper vacuum sealing, not just ziplock bagging, which still has oxygen trapped inside.

It is worth remembering that bacteria naturally present in fish are also adapted to living and growing at cold temperatures, and these will spoil fish more rapidly than bacteria in meat.

Vigilance and planning are important when dealing with fish. It is not advisable to buy fresh fish on a whim, pop it in the fridge and come back to it days later to make something of it.

Ensuring your catch remains fresh

If you catch your own fish, in river, lake or sea, you will know exactly how fresh it is – and if you're going to eat it rather than throw it back you will have to kill it yourself. A good whack on the head with a heavy object should do the job instantly. I always kill fish as they come out of the water – I can't stand the look of a fish gasping away on the beach or riverbank. I gut them when I have a break.

Keeping your catch fresh depends on what you caught and how long the journey home is likely to take. Living in Manchester I found it difficult to get back from my hunting grounds in less than three hours, and consequently I was always looking for ways to be sure my fish was not half cooked in the boot of the car before I got it back.

If it is to be preserved or smoked the fish should be killed, gutted, split open and salted at the point of catching. You don't need much salt to keep fish from spoiling, just enough to give the whole fish a light coating. This is the way I would treat mackerel: a wash in seawater, a light dusting of salt, washed again at home and salted properly before smoking.

An ice box is ideal for fish that you want to cook fresh. I would add a handful of salt to the ice, which reduces the temperature below zero, and then put the fish in the ice box.

An evening's fishing will need a couple of bags of ice in your ice box to start with, salt, and the gutted fish placed on top. If you can get more ice, so much the better: keep on adding ice and salt and, if possible, change the ice at least once. It is a good idea to find a friendly pub to get ice from, either in exchange for some fish or for cash. All-night supermarkets usually sell big bags of ice for about £1.00, which you can use to replenish your ice box on the way home.

Pre-packed and frozen fish

If you are buying pre-packed fresh fish the best way to check for freshness is to see if there is any liquid around the fish and poke it gently to see how springy the flesh is. Any running liquid or un-springy flesh means the fish isn't very fresh and has been losing moisture.

Freezers work at 17°C below zero, which is quite cold enough to keep food safe. But imagine a scenario where some fish is taken from the freezer, pushed around the supermarket for 30 minutes or longer, then left at the checkout because the shopper changed their mind; it may wait another 20 minutes before someone restocks it back in the freezer. It will be partially defrosted – not much, but just a little. So it is important to check frozen fish.

★ Look at the outer packaging, is it frosty? This would indicate that the freezer was not sealed well, so you could not be sure the fish was always deeply frozen.
★ If the packaging is clear, examine the inside of the package for ice crystals. This may indicate that the fish has been partially thawed and then refrozen.
★ Look out for discoloured parts of the fish. This is freezer burn caused by water escaping the flesh and being replaced by oxygen, which affects the colour and texture of the fish. Avoid any discoloured fish.

Choosing fresh seafood

Some people use the term 'seafood' to mean shellfish (mussels, oysters, prawns etc), while to others it means any food from the sea, be it cod, anchovy, crab or squid. We often worry about 'non-fish' seafood being somehow more dangerous than their vertebrate counterparts. It is true that some people develop allergic reactions to certain types of shellfish, but unless you are one of the unlucky ones, there is no reason to avoid these delicious morsels – as long as they are very fresh.

As with fish, there are clues to how fresh the produce is. Most should be labelled with its source and date of harvest. If not, ask the fishmonger when it was caught.

★ Shrimps and prawns – if raw, the flesh should be translucent and shiny; there should be no unpleasant odour.
★ Oysters, mussels, scallops and clams – the shells should look clean and unbroken and should be tightly closed with no gaps. If a shell is slightly open, tap it sharply and it should close instantly: this shows the shellfish are alive and healthy.
★ Lobsters and crabs – should look lively and preferably still swimming in water. If sold boiled, the carapace should be vibrant

and not dull or greying, and it should smell fresh. If you can hold the creature, it should feel heavier than it looks.

★ Frozen seafood should be in undamaged packaging. If there is frost on the inner packaging this can mean it has been slightly defrosted and refrozen; do not buy refrozen goods, whatever they are.

★ Check for freezer burn – discoloured patches that indicate that the food has been in contact with air. It's safe to eat but the texture and flavour will be affected.

The key to good fish

Freshness is of prime importance when it comes to good fish and seafood dishes. Ideally this means having fish that has only just been caught, and kept cold until it is cooked. If you can get fish that is 24 hours old, you will be doing well.

From that starting point you can create a complete image of the sea or the river on a plate. This might sound somewhat romantic, but the absolute joy of the aroma and flavour of the sea is what makes the perfect dish. That exciting explosion of flavours, reminiscent of tides and seaweed, will always make me think of shrimping or standing on a freezing rock fishing for mackerel, codling and sea bass. It is the same with rivers. I can never get over the delight of eating a fresh trout caught that morning, bringing memories of the rise and the beauty of the river, the aroma of water – each river has its own particular fragrance.

CHAPTER 2

How to prepare fish for cooking

If I catch a fish myself, I try to clean it straight away and line the cavity with a little salt before putting the fish on ice. When I buy fish from the fishmonger I usually ask them to clean and descale it for me because it saves time and mess.

The easiest way to start is to buy filleted and skinned fish. However, some people like the skin, which goes crispy when you fry the fish. Leave the skin on and see what you think – but do make sure you remove all the scales. A quick rinse under the cold tap is sufficient preparation but always pat your fish dry with kitchen paper before cooking, even if you are poaching it.

Removing fins and scales

If you find yourself facing a whole fish, the first thing to do is trim off the fins – which can be spiky – using sturdy kitchen scissors.

Most fish, with certain exceptions, such as mackerel, have scales that need to be removed. These are nasty if you get them in your mouth. You can buy a descaler, or alternatively you can use a spoon or a blunt knife. Hold the fish by the tail and rub the edge of the spoon from the tail end towards the head, scraping the scales away as you go. Periodically, give the fish a rinse under cold running water. However, there are times when you don't need to descale:

★ If you are going to cook skinned fillets of fish, it will be easier to remove the skin and scales at the same time – no need to descale it first.
★ If you are going to barbecue a whole fish the scales will protect the flesh as it cooks, and you can peel away the skin and scales before serving.

Cleaning and filleting

Filleting fish is a skill that you will never lose, and it teaches you a lot about the fish you are using.

There are various ways to fillet fish; it partly depends on the type of fish you have.

Ideally you need a filleting knife, which is both sharp and flexible, the more flexible the better. There is a slight curve on the blade and the blade is usually quite thin. I always sharpen my knife before I use it.

I do all of my cleaning and filleting next to the sink, in which there is a container for inedible offcuts – guts and gills – and another for bits for making stock: heads, bones, fins and tail.

CLEANING ROUND FISH

★ First you need to remove the guts. Find the anal vent and insert a short sharp knife. Cut towards the head, keeping the blade level and cutting with a single movement – don't attempt to saw the flesh.

★ Scrape out the guts and discard them. Look along the backbone and remove any organs and blood you find there by scraping gently with the knife.

★ If you are going to cook the fish whole, you may like to leave the head on –but you'll need to remove the gills. With small fish you can just pull them out; for larger fish you'll need a pair of sturdy scissors to cut them out.

★ I usually cut off the head. Make a cut behind the gill opening, cutting through the backbone.

★ Rinse under cold running water and dry with kitchen paper.

FILLETING ROUND FISH

Each fish gives you two fillets.

★ Place your fish on the work surface. Using a filleting knife, make a cut along one side of the backbone so you can feel the knife just touching the bone. Make the cut shallow at first and deepen it with single strokes until you can use your thumb to part the flesh from the bone.

★ Continue making long shallow cuts until the fillet is free.

★ Turn the fish over and repeat for the other side.
★ Rinse the carcass before using for stock.

CLEANING FLATFISH

If you feel the side of the fish, there is a soft side and a firm side. The soft side contains the guts.

★ Cut through the head from the centre point, following the line of the gills. With larger flatfish you might need to use some force, even a mallet.
★ Having cut through half the head, bend the head back and twist it and the guts will come out with the head. If the guts break, get your fingers in and pull the rest out. Discard the guts.
★ Rinse under cold running water and dry with kitchen paper.

FILLETING FLATFISH

Each fish gives you four fillets.

★ Place your fish on the work surface and carefully make a C-shaped cut behind the gills.
★ Using a filleting knife, cut from the first cut along the lateral line visible along the backbone, which is in the centre of the fish. You should feel the backbone on your knife. Continue this cut until you get to the tail, which you can chop off.
★ Starting at the head end and keeping the knife flat, run it along the backbone to the outer edge of the fish with long strokes of the knife, keeping your free hand out of the way, until the fillet comes away.
★ Repeat for the other fillet, then turn the fish over and remove the fillets on the other side.
★ If any of the frill of fins around the outside of the fish remains attached to the fillet, simply trim it off. Some chefs prefer to cut the outer fins off, using a pair of sturdy kitchen scissors, before they start filleting.
★ Rinse the fillets in cold water and dry with kitchen paper.
★ Rinse the carcass before using for stock.

Removing pin bones

No matter how good a filleter you become, there will always be some bones remaining in the fillets. Lay the fillet on a chopping board, skin side down, and run your fingers lightly along the mid line. You will feel the bones peeping out. Catch them with a pair of tweezers or a special pin bone tool until you can no longer feel any.

Removing the skin

You might not always want to remove the skin. I hardly ever remove the skin from salmon fillets, for example: fried in a little oil, the skin is crisp and glorious. Larger whole fish are often baked in their skin; it is then easy to lift the skin off the cooked flesh.

However, there are plenty of recipes when the skin is not needed, such as fish soup or thin fillets of fried fish.

★ Place your fillet skin side up.
★ At the tail end make a small cut, inserting the filleting knife between the skin and the flesh.
★ Grip the skin and flatten the blade under the flesh.
★ Pull back on the skin while at the same time making broad sweeping cuts with the knife. Take your time and don't panic, start sawing or pull too hard.

Preparing prawns, langoustines and crayfish

Because of their comparatively small size, live shrimp, prawns, langoustines and crayfish are killed within a second of immersion in boiling water. I use a large pan of water, salted and at a rolling boil.

Once cooked, which takes only a minute or so, they change colour. Drain them and leave to cool. Remove the head by twisting it off and the legs by pulling them away. Slip your thumb under the shell to remove it.

In all but the smallest shrimp and prawns you will see a dark line in the flesh, which is the digestive canal. It isn't poisonous, but it's best to cut it out. Simply slice along the back and tease out the tract; you may need to rinse the prawns under cold running water, then pat dry.

UNCOOKED PRAWNS AND LANGOUSTINES

If a recipe calls for raw prawns or langoustines, you can clean them before cooking by twisting off the head, pulling off the legs and forcing off the shell. Look for the dark intestinal canal and pull it out.

Preparing crabs and lobsters

There is a lot of debate about the best way to kill these animals, and humane killing is the order of the day. It is difficult to write about this because I would not wish to encourage people into methods that cause difficulty for the animal.

Many people just throw the live crab or lobster into a large pan of boiling water, and wait for it to be cooked, ignoring its attempts to get out of the pan. Some people prefer to put the live animal in the freezer for a couple of hours until it becomes still and unconscious, then pop it into boiling water. Actually, a large crab or lobster at 0°C will cool down the boiling water enough to wake the animal, and death is not instant. Crabs shed their claws in these conditions and often in such a way that the flavour is ruined.

More recently, the prescribed method has been to freeze the animal for a couple of hours and then kill it by stabbing.

All these methods have some doubt associated with them, and I would say that for the majority of dishes I make I buy ready prepared crab and lobster, which have been stunned by the only method proven to really work – electrical stunning, beyond the capabilities of the average kitchen. However, I use the cooling/stabbing method whenever I need really fresh meat.

KILLING BY STABBING

Cool the animal in the freezer for a couple of hours. Make sure the claws are secured so the animal can't nip you.

★ **For a crab**, you will need a sturdy pointed screwdriver. There are two nerve centres, one at the back and one at the front. Once you damage these the crab is said to be dead. Place the crab on its back, lift the flap at the back underside of the crab and you will see a conical indentation. Force a screwdriver into the centre of this area, right the way through. Then immediately repeat the process through the mouth of the crab, between the eyes. This process can take a minute or so, and you need to be accurate and efficient.

★ Unless your recipe calls for raw crabmeat, you can now cook the crab in a large pan of salted boiling water. Allow approximately 12 minutes per kg, but don't double the time for larger crabs; add 3–4 minutes for every extra 500g. Drain and leave to cool, but don't use cold water to speed up cooling time or it will make the crabmeat watery.

★ For instructions on preparing a crab, see the recipe for Dressed crab in chapter 7.

★ **For a lobster**, you will need a large, sharp knife, strong enough to cut through the hard shell. Place the animal on its front and plunge a large knife into the thorax (the top part of the shell), about 2–3cm from the front of its head. Push the knife down and cut forwards, dividing the head in two.

★ Cook the lobster in a large pan of salted boiling water. Allow 15 minutes for a 750g lobster; for larger lobsters, add about 5 minutes for every extra 500g. Drain and leave to cool.

★ For instructions on preparing a lobster, see the recipe for Lobster Thermidor in chapter 7.

Preparing mussels and clams

On the whole, shellfish need little preparation apart from making sure they are still alive and as fresh as they can be.

Bivalve shellfish, that is creatures with two half shells, should be tightly closed before cooking, indicating that they are still alive. Any open shells should be tested: tap them on the work surface and they should close; if they remain open, discard them. Discard any shellfish with cracked shells.

Always give the shells a good rinse under cold running water. Scrub or scrape the shells if necessary to remove any barnacles or seaweed. Most mussels these days are farmed, and after harvesting are kept in tanks of fresh water to remove grit and excess saltiness. If you have wild mussels, soak them in fresh water for 30 minutes.

Some shellfish, mussels in particular, have 'beards' or byssal threads, which have to be removed – just grab and tug them off. It's not that they are poisonous, they are just a little unpalatable.

Preparing oysters

Unless you've had lots of practice, oysters can be difficult to prepare and you need to protect yourself. Wear an apron, and fold a large tea towel to protect your gripping hand. You need a good oyster knife, which is blunt and short, with a protective guard above the blade.

★ Wrap the curved shell of the oyster in the folded towel, making sure there's plenty of protection for your hand – I'm right-handed, so for me I hold the oyster in my left hand. Hold the oyster on the work surface with the hinged end nearest you.

★ On the hinge there is a tiny gap. Insert the oyster knife (with quite a bit of wiggling and very controlled pushing) and, once inside, twist the knife firmly but gently to open the shell.

★ Prise the shells apart, keeping the lower shell level to keep in all the juices. If the flesh is still attached to the top shell, scrape it free with the knife.

★ Remove any broken shell and run the knife underneath the oyster to cut it free.

Preparing scallops

Scallops are often sold ready prepared; if not, you can ask the fishmonger to prepare them for you and save the shells if your recipe suggests serving the scallops in their shells. If you want to have a go yourself, working with scallops requires two knives: an oyster knife and a filleting knife. You should hold the scallop in a folded tea towel to protect your hand, as for oysters.

★ Insert the oyster knife through the hinge and twist firmly but gently to open the shell.

★ Insert the filleting knife and slide it along the flat side of the shell, keeping the knife in contact with the shell, to detach the flesh.

★ Using the oyster knife again, open the shell and remove the scallop meat. Discard the black stomach sac and the frilly bit around the edge. You will be left with a disc of pure white flesh and a curved coral, orange at the top and light brown at the base. Trim off any other unidentifiable bits and pieces and discard.

★ Briefly rinse the flesh and roe and dry with kitchen paper.

Cuttlefish, squid and octopus

Fundamentally there isn't a great deal of difference between the three. Cuttlefish are generally the smallest, about 20–25cm long. Like squid, they have eight small tentacles and two longer tentacles for catching prey. The most common edible squid around the British Isles can grow up to 60cm long, although you'll usually find them about half that size. The octopus is the largest, with eight large, meaty tentacles – it can grow quite large but the ones sold for cooking are usually about 30–40cm long. Baby octopus, about 7cm long, are increasingly common; you are more likely to find them in supermarkets and there are even suggestions that battered baby octopus will replace fish and chips!

The flesh of these animals provides a firm but delicate texture and a creamy sea flavour, which are both easily ruined by poor cooking, leaving your food hard, rubbery and tasteless. For best results they can be cooked low and slow, or very hot and quickly.

When preparing these animals, beware of the ink, which can stain clothes and work surfaces, so **do the initial preparation and cleaning in the sink**. However, these days many fishmongers clean them before sale.

PREPARING CUTTLEFISH AND SQUID

★ You will find a head end (with tentacles) that fits into the body (sometimes referred to as a 'tube' or 'mantle'). Take hold of both sections and with a twist and pull, remove the head. The guts – which may include the ink sac – should come out attached to the head. Among the guts in squid you should find a transparent quill or pen. In cuttlefish there is a chalky white structure that you'll need to pull out. Use your fingers to feel inside the body and gently pull out any remaining innards.

★ If you want to use the ink in a recipe, you can remove the ink sac (a small grey or blue pouch with a white outer membrane) and carefully squeeze the ink into a cup. If you damage it, just wash the ink away; it will not harm the meat.

★ Cut the tentacles away. You can do this in two ways, depending on the size of the squid and on personal preference. Either cut off individual tentacles, or cut off the front of the head, just below the eyes. In this case you will also need to remove the hard beak – just pop it out using your thumb. Give the tentacles a quick rinse and pat dry.

★ Remove the purplish outer skin from the body by making a small incision at the fin end and pulling it away under cold running water. Turn the body inside out, rinse well and dry with kitchen paper.

★ If you want squid rings, slice the rings while the body is inside out. Alternatively, if you are going to grill or flash-fry your squid, slice open the body to give you two sheets. Using a small sharp knife, score the inside with diagonal cross-cuts, which will keep the meat flat when cooked. You could also cut the meat into strips.

PREPARING OCTOPUS

Octopus, especially the larger ones, are best cooked either very quickly – for example by flash frying or barbecuing – or very slowly, for example in a casserole.

★ An octopus has a membrane that joins the body/head and tentacles: cut this with a sharp knife, separating the tentacles.

★ Turn the head inside out and remove the innards. Rinse under cold running water. Remove the beak, which needs a little pressure.

★ Turn the head back the right way and pull away the skin. This is sometimes easier to do if it is dipped into boiling water for a couple of seconds and then run under cold water.

★ Cut out the eyes; it's easiest to cut the head away from the eyes altogether.

★ If you are frying, grilling or barbecuing the octopus, slit the body up one side and open it out flat, then score the inside in a diamond pattern, using a sharp knife. Alternatively, cut into slices.

★ Clean the tentacles in cold water, removing any dirt from the suckers. For flash frying, slice the tentacles into bite-sized chunks.

CHAPTER 3

Cooking fish, the basics

Cooking fish is sometimes thought of as being difficult, and so it might, since there is such a wide range of creatures that fall under the umbrella of 'fish'. However, the best way to cook most fish is simply, and you will soon gain the experience to know when something is right. There's only one rule to remember: don't overcook it.

There are certain basic methods of cooking fish that have stood the test of time. The vast majority of fish recipes are based on these methods, with variations as people push the boundaries of experience, discovering methods from around the world, following up on new technology, and rediscovering old ways.

Why fish cooks quickly

Fish cooks quickly and is an excellent 'fast' food. It can be fried, poached, steamed, grilled/barbecued or oven roasted. Never overcook fish, though, as it loses flavour and texture. The reason for this can be explained by considering the difference between, say, a lamb steak and something of similar size, such as a salmon steak. Although they are roughly the same bulk, a lamb steak takes longer to cook than an equivalent salmon steak. This is because mammal muscle is a lot denser, with a great many more fibres than fish meat.

The land animal is always working against gravity: standing, walking, eating, even sleeping. Movement requires specialist muscles, usually in antagonistic pairs, to physically pick up and move a large part of the body. Consequently, land animal muscles are dense, held together with lots of collagen, and the fibres are long and interconnected.

Fish, on the other hand, has much of its bulk supported by water. Movement is a question of pushing against the liquid, which gives only a little resistance, allowing the fish to get along with few muscles for locomotion. The muscle fibres are much less dense, and the collagen fibres are correspondingly short.

When the fish and meat are cooked, collagen is converted to gelatine, among other things, and dissolves, leaving the coagulated muscle proteins in flakes.

How to tell when fish is cooked

Generally, fish is cooked when the flesh is opaque. Undercooked fish has flakes that are still translucent, overcooked fish has flakes falling apart. The time between these two states can be just a minute or so, so fish should not be left alone, you need to watch it as it cooks. Test by gently inserting the tip of a knife into the thickest part of the fish so that you can see the flesh is opaque all the way through.

Overcooked fish will be tasteless and falling apart; overcooked shellfish will be rubbery – the inevitable result of too much heat. But at the same time you want all the muscle to be cooked through, no slimy, translucent, raw bits.

Grilling

This is a perfect way to cook fish, either under the grill or on a barbecue. It is ideal for any fish or fillet that is more than 2–3cm thick. Thin fillets are not really suitable for the fierce heat of the grill – although shellfish are wonderful with just a few minutes of fierce heat.

It is a good idea to make sure the grill (or baking tray) is really clean, to prevent the fish from sticking. A palette knife is useful for turning the fish. On a barbecue, use a metal spatula.

Start by making cuts into the flesh. This is particularly useful for sardines and mackerel, but any fish will benefit from this. It allows the heat to get quickly into the centre of the fish and also caramelises the cut edges for added flavour.

Line a baking tray (if using) with foil and heat the grill or barbecue to high. Brush the fillets with oil or melted butter and place on the baking tray or directly on the grill rack. Season with a little salt and pepper. Place under the grill or on the barbecue, not too close to the heat source, and cook for about 4 minutes depending on how thick the fillets are.

Carefully turn the fish and cook for 2–3 minutes on the other side. Generally, about 8–10 minutes per 2–3cm of fish is ideal. If you cook whole fish you can look inside the cavity to judge how well the meat is cooked.

Leave the fish to rest on a warmed plate for a few minutes before serving.

Frying

Shallow frying, or pan frying as it is often called these days, is quick and easy. This is ideal for fillets and for smallish whole fish such as herring and trout.

Place a tablespoon or two of plain flour in a dish and season with salt and pepper. Dip each fillet in the seasoned flour.

Heat 2 tablespoons of oil in a frying pan and put the fillets into the hot oil, skin side down if you are keeping the skin on, and fry over a high heat for about 3 minutes.

Don't be tempted to put too much fish in the pan as this reduces the temperature of the oil and the fish will not cook evenly.

Turn the fish over carefully and cook for 3 more minutes or until the fish is done. It is cooked when the flesh is opaque and the flakes separate when loosened with a fork. Don't overcook as the fish will separate and become difficult to remove from the pan.

Deep frying is suitable for small fish, larger fish cut into small fillets, squid and prawns. They are usually coated in seasoned flour or batter before frying.

Poaching

You can poach fish in almost any liquid, and the resulting fishy liquor is ideal for making a sauce to serve with the fish (see chapter 10). Trout poached in water with cider is wonderful, as is almost any white fish in white wine. However, you have to be careful not to overcook the fish, so the key word is gentle: simmer, don't boil. You can poach fillets or whole fish; the timing depends on the thickness of the fish.

Place the fish in lightly salted water or milk to just cover the fish and bring to the boil, then immediately turn down the heat to a very gentle simmer for 4–8 minutes, depending on the size of the fish. The flesh should become opaque and cooked through but not falling apart. Carefully lift the fish out of the liquor and drain it briefly, keeping the liquor to make a sauce if you wish.

You need a decent-sized wide pan for poaching, but it needn't be huge unless you intend to poach whole fish such as large trout or salmon, for which a fish kettle is traditional. To be honest, my fish kettle got used for hot smoking (see chapter 6).

Steaming

Steaming your fish is the ultimate in healthy eating. You needn't use any fat, though I tend to oil the fillets, place them in a steamer basket and season lightly with salt and pepper. Bring the water to the boil, then put the fish in the steamer basket on top and steam for 4–8 minutes depending on the size of the fillets. Smallish whole fish can also be steamed; this will take a little longer. You can add aromatics – such as spring onions, star anise, sliced ginger or lemongrass – to your steaming liquid or sprinkle these over the fish.

Mussels and clams are often 'steamed' in a large pan over a high heat, covered with a lid; it takes just a few minutes for the shells to open. For extra flavour you can add finely chopped onion or shallot and a splash of wine or cider to the pan before adding the shellfish.

Roasting

Not many people realise that fish can be roasted (baked at high temperature) in the oven. This method is especially suited to meaty fish such as cod and hake, but it is good for most fish and intensifies the flavour.

Preheat the oven to 200°C/gas mark 6. Brush the fish with oil and place on a baking sheet or in a roasting pan. Cook for 8–12 minutes or until the flesh is opaque and the flakes separate when they are loosened with a fork.

To give extra texture, you can crisp the skin side of the fish by frying before roasting. One of the advantages of roasting fish is you can add other ingredients to the pan, such as tomatoes, peppers or potatoes, and the cooking juices will infuse the whole dish with flavour.

Baking in parcels

An excellent way to cook fish is wrapping in a foil or greaseproof paper parcel (in tropical countries a banana leaf is sometimes used). The fish will steam in its own juices, so there is no need for any extra liquid.

Preheat the oven to 220°C/gas mark 7. Place each fillet (or small whole fish, such as trout) on a piece of foil or greaseproof paper and season lightly with salt and pepper. Place a knob of butter or a glug of olive oil on top of the fish. Add a sprig of parsley or dill or a slice of lemon if you like. Fold the foil or paper securely round the fish and place in a roasting pan or ovenproof dish. Cook for 15–20 minutes.

Microwave

People throw everything in the microwave these days. It can be a good way to cook fish, so long as you do it slowly. You can't just pop it in on full power, go away and expect to return to perfectly cooked fish when the bell dings. I have used the microwave for fillets, fish steaks and small whole fish, but I don't cook shellfish in the microwave because they can quickly become rubbery.

Use a low power setting, cook for a minute and then check, continuing to cook and check until the flesh is just perfectly cooked to your liking. Then – and this is important – leave it to rest for 1–3 minutes (depending on the thickness of the fish) before serving.

CHAPTER 4

Sea fish

It has often been said, and indeed sung, that there are plenty more fish in the sea. Alas, this is no longer true, and very careful management of sea fishing is now an important part of our food chain.

What amazes me is that the waters around the UK are home to a wealth of fish and other edible sea creatures, loved all the world over, yet these are often ignored by the inhabitants of our islands. The quality of our fish is probably the best in the world. There are a number of reasons for this. Firstly, the maritime climate of the UK is cool but not so cold as to freeze the inshore bays. The cooler water is, the more oxygen it contains, and consequently the seas around Britain are packed with oxygen. Secondly, the seas are rich with nutrients deposited by the innumerable rivers. These nutrients feed plankton, tiny organisms that form the first link in the marine food chain. If you feed on plankton, British waters are the place to be! It is rumoured that the Romans invaded the islands because of the seafood.

In the late twentieth and early twenty-first centuries, former culinary staples such as herrings, sardines, mullet, sild, mackerel and whiting have lost popularity. Nowadays we only seem interested in fish we can treat like a steak!

However, many of the fish we reject just happen to be the most healthy, and perhaps the most flavoursome too. Eating fish, especially oily fish such as herring and mackerel, is good for you beyond more or less any other food or medicine. These fish contain omega-3 oils that help in so many ways that a weekly dose of them is really important in maintaining a healthy heart and brain, good joints, a great complexion and general good health. But perhaps the best reason for eating fish and seafood of all kinds is that it tastes wonderful.

Anchovies

The anchovy resembles a sardine in looks and flavour, and is mostly caught in the Mediterranean. In the UK it is usually found salted, filleted and packed in oil (in a tin or a jar), which has to be drained. You can also buy anchovies cured in large containers if you need larger amounts. Preserved anchovies are the condiment of the seafood world, and are an ingredient of Worcestershire sauce and Gentleman's Relish.

If you see fresh anchovies for sale, the best way to cook them is to toss them in seasoned flour and deep- or shallow-fry them; they are eaten whole, in the same way as whitebait.

If you search the internet for anchovy recipes you will find sauces, salads (Caesar and Niçoise) and pizza – as if the anchovy isn't really an ingredient in its own right. However, it is the basis for some excellent dishes and with a little imagination something amazing lies just the other side of the cooker.

Anchovy butter

This is so simple and makes a brilliant condiment to top plain grilled fish, add to roast beef or lamb, or simply spread on bread. You can add some of this when making pâté for an extra tang, stuff some into olives for topping a pizza or use it to cook onions.

30g anchovy fillets, drained
125g butter (unsalted is best because the anchovy is rich in salt)

1 Place the anchovies and butter in a blender and whiz.
2 Spoon into a container and keep in the fridge for at least a day before use.

Anchovy crust for roast lamb

Lamb and anchovies may sound an unlikely pairing, but as the lamb cooks the fishiness disappears, leaving a rich savoury flavour.

FOR 1 ROASTING JOINT
handful of rosemary, finely chopped
1 tbsp chopped fresh mint
1 tbsp chopped fresh sage or ½tbsp dried sage
2 garlic cloves, crushed and chopped
6 anchovy fillets, drained
4 tbsp sunflower oil

1 Put all the herbs, garlic and anchovies together in a mortar and pestle or a small bowl and mix to a paste with the oil.
2 Spread evenly over the upper surface of the lamb joint and roast for the required time.

Roast anchovy peppers

**This lovely dish is brilliant on toast. Serve as a first course or
a lunch dish with a side salad.**

SERVES 4
4 large red peppers
16 green olives – or more if you like
2 onions, thinly sliced
8 garlic cloves, crushed and finely chopped
30g anchovy fillets, drained
125–200g feta cheese, crumbled
olive oil for drizzling

1 Preheat the oven to 200°C/gas mark 6.
2 Cut the peppers in half and remove the seeds and pith. Slice the
   olives into quarters.
3 Place the peppers on a baking sheet. Divide the onions among the
   pepper halves, then top with the olives, garlic and anchovy fillets.
   Sprinkle feta over each half pepper. Drizzle with olive oil.
4 Bake for 20 minutes. Serve warm or cold.

Pissaladière

This is a dish from Nice in southern France. It's similar to a pizza, but with no tomatoes. Essentially it is a purée of onions, garlic and herbs on a pastry base, topped with a lattice of anchovies, dotted with black olives. Some recipes call for a yeasted pizza dough, others for a deeper bread base, but most people think of this as more a tart than a pizza.

SERVES 4–6
4 tbsp olive oil
5 onions, very finely sliced
4 garlic cloves, crushed and chopped
3 sprigs of fresh thyme leaves, chopped
salt and pepper
350g puff pastry
50g tin of anchovy fillets, drained
lots of olives – black and tasty ones!

1 Preheat the oven to 180°C/gas mark 4.
2 Put the olive oil, onions, garlic and thyme in a heavy-bottomed pan over a low heat and cook slowly for 20 minutes until really soft, stirring often. You do not want the mixture to caramelise, but it must be cooked enough for the onions to form a mush. Season to taste with pepper and a little salt.
3 Roll out the puff pastry to a rectangle, place it on a baking tray, and fold over the edges to make a small lip around the outside. Bake for 20–25 minutes.
4 Drain the onion mixture and spread the onion pulp over the pastry. Arrange the anchovies on top (a trellis pattern is traditional), then dot the olives between the anchovies. Bake for 10–12 minutes. Serve warm or cold.

Jansson's temptation

Some say this dish was named for an actor, others that it was named after a film. It is essentially a Swedish casserole which was originally made with pickled sprats. The appearance of anchovy might have been because of a mistranslation of the Swedish word for pickled sprats, *ansjovis*.

SERVES 6

2 tbsp olive oil
2 large onions, diced
100g anchovy fillets, drained
6 medium potatoes (approx. 1kg), peeled and sliced thinly lengthways
salt and pepper
400ml double cream

1 Preheat the oven to 200°C/gas mark 6.
2 Heat the oil in a frying pan and cook the onions until just browning.
3 In a baking dish, layer one-third of the onions, one-third of the anchovies and one-third of the potatoes. Season each layer of ingredients with pepper and a little salt (remember that the anchovies are salty). Repeat the layers until everything is used up.
4 Pour over the cream to cover the whole dish and bake for 1 hour. Serve with fish, or just on its own.

Peacock's temptation

This is something we like at home; inspired by Jansson's offering, but decidedly different, with no cream. However, if you fancy pushing the boat out, by all means add some cream.

SERVES 4

500g new potatoes
2 large onions, roughly diced
2–3 garlic cloves, crushed and chopped
1 red pepper, finely chopped
100g anchovy fillets, drained
250g Cheddar cheese, grated

1 Preheat the oven to 180°C/gas mark 4.
2 Boil the potatoes in their skins with the onions and garlic for 5 minutes.
3 Drain and cut the potatoes into 1cm pieces.
4 In a baking dish, layer the ingredients in the following order: potatoes; onions and garlic; more potatoes; red pepper; anchovies; cheese. Bake for 35 minutes. Serve hot.

Cod

The cod is an amazing animal that can grow into a huge fish. There are various types of cod, the most important being the Atlantic cod, the Pacific cod and the Greenland cod. The largest fish can be up to 2 metres in length, but normally cod are about half this size.

Stocks of the Atlantic cod are officially classed as vulnerable. Quota systems have improved the picture somewhat, but there is much more to be done before the population of cod attains the levels of the 1950s. Some Pacific cod and cod from certain fisheries are certified as sustainable by the MSC – with cod it's particularly important to look for the MSC logo.

However, there is no better fish for frying, and the mild white flesh is very satisfying to eat.

Eating cod shouldn't be a problem, so long as we don't eat it to the exclusion of all other fish in the sea. Diversity is the key to sustainability.

Mustard roast cod

This is a brilliant dish, which I think originated in the United States. I've tweaked the original recipe to use double cream instead of crème fraiche.

SERVES 4

25g butter, plus extra for greasing
50g shallots, finely chopped
4 thick cod fillets
1 tbsp mustard seeds
1 tbsp English mustard
250ml double cream
salt and pepper

1 Preheat the oven to 200°C/gas mark 6. Butter a large ovenproof dish.
2 Heat the butter in a frying pan and gently sweat the shallots until translucent.
3 Place the fish fillets in the buttered dish, skin side down.
4 Once the shallots have softened, add the mustard seeds, the mustard and the cream, stirring all the time to avoid splitting. Season to taste.
5 Pour the mixture over the cod and bake for 15 minutes.

Battered cod

We used to go to a chip shop and buy cod and chips and then ask for some scrapings to eat on the way home. These were the bits of batter that fell off in the fryer; they were wonderful with salt and vinegar, and were given to us free.

My friend at the 'chippy' made his batter in a big bucket with nothing more than plain flour and water. This recipe includes some cornflour for a slightly lighter batter and has stood the test of time. However, there are always trends in cooking, and these days people often use beer instead of water for the batter, with spices to add flavour and colour.

Instead of cod, try this with another, more sustainable member of the cod family, such as pollack or coley.

SERVES 2–4
oil for deep frying
2–4 cod fillets, about 180–200g each
2–4 tbsp plain flour for dusting

Batter
50g self-raising flour
50g cornflour
generous pinch of salt
1 tsp turmeric, curry powder or garlic purée (optional)
150ml cold water, sparkling water or beer

1 To make the batter, combine the flour, cornflour, salt and your chosen flavouring, if using, in a bowl. Add the water or beer – or use half water, half beer – and beat with a wooden spoon until you have a smooth, lump-free batter. Place in the fridge for an hour to rest.

2 Before using, give the batter a final stir. Heat the oil in a deep frying pan – it is hot enough when a drizzle of batter in the oil sets and cooks within a second or so.

3 Pat the fillets dry with kitchen paper and then dust in a little flour before dunking in the batter. Let some of the batter drip back into the bowl: you don't need too much.

4 Gently lower the fish into the hot oil and cook for 6–8 minutes, depending on the thickness of the fillet.

5 Lift the fish out of the oil and drain on a couple of layers of kitchen paper before serving with chips and plenty of salt and vinegar.

Ajoarriero

This is a northern Spanish dish from the Basque Country and is said to have been popularised by mule drivers who needed an easy dish on the mad dash to get their animals to market before the competition. Originally made from salted cod, the dish is basically a ragout of peppers, tomatoes and garlic. It is very garlicky – you might wish to reduce the garlic. The colours of white, red and green reflect the Basque flag, which is a feature of much of the cuisine of the area.

SERVES 6

2 tbsp olive oil
1 large onion, finely chopped
5 garlic cloves: 2 whole, 3 chopped
2 large potatoes, peeled and cubed
1 green and 1 red pepper, deseeded and cut into thin strips
500g chopped fresh tomatoes or 400g canned chopped tomatoes
salt and pepper
800g cod, cut into 5cm strips

1 Heat the oil in a decent-sized wide pan and add the onion and garlic.
2 Put the potatoes into a pan of salted boiling water and boil until tender.
3 When the onion is translucent, add the peppers, stir in and cook for a minute. Add the tomatoes and cook for a further 3 minutes over a moderate heat. Season to taste.
4 Lay the cod on the top of this sauce and cook for about 5 minutes.
5 Check the potatoes are soft before draining. Add the potatoes to the pan with the fish and gently stir in.
6 Cook for a further 10 minutes over a low heat. Serve with crusty bread and/or salad.

Cajun-spiced cod

The state of Louisiana in the southern USA has a troubled history. It was colonised by the French, then the Spanish, then went back into French hands, and was finally bought by the United States in 1803. The huge slave population added an African element to the cooking and the cuisine reflects these considerable influences.

Make the spice rub in advance and store in a sealed container: it will keep for at least a year. The amount given here is enough for many applications: why not try it on other fish, or on chicken or pork chops?

SERVES 2
2 cod fillets, about 200g each
4 tbsp olive oil
3 tbsp Cajun spice rub
lemon wedges to serve

Cajun spice rub
5 tbsp sweet paprika
2 tbsp onion powder
2 tbsp garlic powder
2 tbsp dried oregano
1 tbsp dried thyme
1 tbsp crushed black pepper
1 tbsp white pepper
1 tbsp cayenne pepper
1 tbsp salt
1 tbsp celery seeds

1 To make the spice rub, place all the ingredients in a bowl and mix very thoroughly. Store in a lidded container.
2 When you are ready to cook, wash and dry the fillets, then rub the

fish on both sides with half the olive oil. Add the spice rub and gently massage in.

3 Add the remaining oil to a hot frying pan and cook the fish for 4 minutes on each side or until cooked through.

4 Serve with lemon wedges. In Louisiana this is generally served with rice and greens.

Torsk

Torsk is the Danish, Norwegian and Swedish word for 'cod'. But the word has become mostly associated with a dish of poached cod, usually served with potatoes or salad. When it comes to the grilling stage, don't have the grill too hot: you don't want the fish to disintegrate, just to flake easily with the fork. For extra flavour you can add half a glass of dry vermouth to the poaching liquid, once the mixture is boiling.

SERVES 2

600ml water
600ml whole milk
1 tbsp black peppercorns
1 tbsp salt
1 onion, chopped
2 carrots, roughly chopped
2–3 potatoes, roughly chopped
handful of fresh parsley, chopped
2 skinless cod fillets
25g butter, melted

1 Put the water and milk into a pan and bring to the boil. Add the peppercorns, salt, onion, carrots, potatoes and parsley and boil for 10 minutes.
2 Place the cod fillets in a glass or earthenware dish and pour the hot liquor and the vegetables over the fish. Leave to stand for 10 minutes. Preheat the grill to moderate.
3 Carefully remove the fish and dry with kitchen paper.
4 Brush the fish on both sides with melted butter and grill for 3 minutes each side under moderate heat.
5 Meanwhile, using a slotted spoon, lift the potatoes, carrots and onion out of the poaching liquid, and place on warmed plates. Add the grilled fish and serve immediately.

Cod loin with creamy spinach and spicy dressing

White fish and mild spices go down a treat, and this dressing is an easy way to serve a spicy sauce with cod.

Cod loin is a strange term. Obviously the loin of pork or beef is well known to us: we can find the muscle on the back of the animal. So where is it in a fish? It isn't. Large fish such as cod have fillets that are thinner at either end, and thicker in the middle. The loin is from the centre, the thickest part of the fillet, and is considered to be the best part.

SERVES 4
4 cod loin fillets, about 180–200g each
1–2 tbsp olive oil
about 600g spinach
salt and pepper
about 4 tbsp crème fraîche

Spicy dressing
2 tsp clear honey
2 tsp tomato purée
1 garlic clove, chopped
½ tsp paprika
¼ tsp cayenne pepper
1 tsp hot curry powder
few dashes of Worcestershire sauce
4 tsp soy sauce
2 tsp sesame oil
5 tbsp olive oil
5 tbsp lemon juice

1 Coat the fish with a little olive oil and place in a single layer in a steamer. Once the steam is being produced, cook the fish for about 6 minutes, depending on the thickness of the fish.

2 While the fish is cooking, prepare the creamy spinach. Plunge the spinach into a pan of boiling water, leave for about 30 seconds, then drain well and squeeze out the excess water, using a ladle to push the spinach down in your colander. Place the spinach in a bowl and season to taste. Stir in the crème fraîche and keep warm.

3 To make the dressing, put all the ingredients into a small pan and heat until just hot, then remove from the heat.

4 Divide the spinach among four warmed plates and place a piece of fish on top. Spoon 2 tablespoons of the dressing on top of the fish and serve.

Miso cod

It is hardly possible to write about cod without including
a Japanese recipe using miso. This wonderful ingredient,
fermented soybean paste, has been used to make soup and to
flavour other dishes for thousands of years. There are many
types of miso, perhaps the most popular being akamiso, an
aged, dark red version. You can buy miso paste from Chinese
stores and specialist supermarkets, and it keeps well in a
sealed container in the fridge.

You will need to marinate the fish for two days. I make this
dish in vacuum-sealed bags: it's a great way to marinate food.

SERVES 4
4 cod fillets, skin on

Miso marinade
300ml sake (rice wine)
4 tbsp dark miso paste – or any type of miso you can get
2–3 spring onions, finely chopped
30g granulated sugar
5g fresh ginger, grated

1 To make the marinade, bring the sake to the boil in a pan and add the
   miso, spring onions, sugar and ginger, stirring well until the miso
   has dissolved, then boil for about 5 minutes. Leave to cool.
2 Pour the marinade over the cod fillets. You can use any container for
   this; I find vacuum-bags are the easiest, but a covered container is
   just as good. Leave in the fridge for two days to marinate.
3 When you are ready to cook, preheat the oven to 200°C/gas mark 6.
4 Remove the fish and carefully pat dry, discarding the marinade.
   Place in a baking dish and bake for 15 minutes. Serve with rice and/
   or salad.

Coley

Coley used to be boiled and fed to cats: they loved it. But it is gradually becoming more popular in the kitchen. Coley is the least expensive fish on the market, so you can experiment with it without breaking the bank.

In some parts of the country it is known as saithe. Pollack is closely related to coley, and both are members of the cod family. They can grow to over a metre in length and weigh up to 20kg.

Coley and pollack are excellent alternatives to cod, which they resemble in texture and flavour. Coley's slightly grey flesh has put people off eating it, but it lightens when cooked and in fact it is really good eating. Consequently, any recipes for cod or haddock will be served just as well with coley or pollack, and they are excellent ingredients for fish pie. It goes to show how often our choice of food is dictated by how it looks. If the flesh was whiter, it would be a much more valuable fish.

In northern Europe coley is smoked, when it gains a yellowish colour, and is sold as sea salmon, though it is not related to salmon.

Steamed coley with chilli dipping sauce

I eat this dish using chopsticks to pull the fish into small pieces and dip them into the sauce, which is served separately, in a small bowl.

SERVES 2
2 coley fillets
1 spring onion, finely chopped
2 tbsp soy sauce
2 tbsp chilli sauce
1 tbsp white wine vinegar
pinch of salt

1 Place the coley fillets in a steamer and cook for about 12 minutes, until the fish is cooked through.
2 Meanwhile, mix the spring onion, soy sauce, chilli sauce, vinegar and salt in a bowl. Serve separately.

Coley with tomato and basil dressing

This is a really lovely way to serve coley. It has a summery Mediterranean feel and is very healthy.

SERVES 2

4 tbsp olive oil
2 coley fillets
2 shallots, finely chopped
2 garlic cloves, finely chopped
3–4 plum tomatoes, deseeded and finely chopped
20g green or black olives, washed and sliced
2 tbsp white wine vinegar
30g fresh basil, chopped
salt and pepper

1 Heat half the olive oil in a frying pan and fry the fish for a few minutes, turning once, until cooked through. Set aside.
2 Add the remaining oil to a saucepan and heat the shallots and garlic for about 30 seconds. Add the tomatoes, olives, vinegar and basil and warm through. Season to taste.
3 Spoon the dressing over the fish and serve with a green salad.

Dogfish

This is a member of the shark family, and is often sold as rock salmon or huss. You can see dogfish swimming about under jetties and piers; it grows up to 75cm long. It has disappeared from the table in recent years, but it is as good as any white fish. It has pinkish flesh but very good flakes.

The great thing about dogfish is that it is boneless, with just a central spinal cartilage. Some people simply slice the cleaned fish into steaks, but I don't like to mess about with these steaks on the plate, and I always feel it is a waste of sauce. I prefer to fillet the fish. The skin has no scales but it can be tough; I usually leave it on to protect the fish as it cooks, and it is easy to pull off once the fish is done.

Fried rock salmon cubes

I discovered this recipe on the World Sea Fishing forum. It is really excellent – and so simple. If you have a deep fat fryer you can judge the cooking just right.

1 Skin the fillets and cut the flesh into bite-sized pieces. Coat with seasoned flour and deep fry for 2 minutes. Some people dip the fish pieces in egg and breadcrumbs. Alternatively, you could dip them in a batter (see page 34).
2 Serve with lemon wedges and salad.

Baked rock salmon fillets in tomato

This is adapted from a recipe I found on the internet: the original had more herbs, but I didn't particularly like them all, so I reduced the amount.

SERVES 2

25g butter

1 large onion, finely chopped

2 garlic cloves, crushed and chopped

1 green pepper, chopped

500g chopped fresh tomatoes or 400g canned chopped tomatoes

1 tbsp chopped chives, or a chopped spring onion

handful of fresh parsley, chopped

approx. 70ml dry white wine or fish stock

salt and pepper

4 dogfish fillets

1 potato, thinly sliced

1 Preheat the oven to 200°C/gas mark 6.
2 Put the butter, onion and garlic in a frying pan over a low heat and sweat until the onion is translucent.
3 Add the green pepper and cook for 2 minutes, then add the tomatoes and herbs and slowly bring to the boil.
4 Assess how much liquid you have from the tomatoes and add a little wine or fish stock to make it wet but not like soup. Season to taste.
5 Put a layer of this mixture into a baking dish, arrange the fish on top and then cover with the rest of the tomato mixture.
6 Layer the potato slices thinly over the top and bake for 20–30 minutes.

Dover sole

Dover sole is popular because it has a lovely flavour, delicate but firm meat and, possibly more importantly, it lifts away from the bone more easily than almost any other fish.

Most Dover soles are 30–40cm long and weigh about 250–350g. A larger one will feed two people.

It is a long thin flatfish with a brown upper skin; this is usually removed before cooking. To do this, make an incision halfway through the fish at the tail and peel back a flap of the skin. You will need a tea towel to grip the skin and pull it away, while holding down the tail end. Be careful around the head, if you want to keep it on. The pale underside is usually descaled before cooking. You can cut off the 'wings' – the frill of fins around the outside of the fish – with a pair of scissors.

Dover sole is best cooked as simply as possible.

Grilled Dover sole

This is the classic way to cook Dover sole, and it couldn't be easier.

1 All you need to do is to clean and prepare one Dover sole per person and season the skinned side with salt and pepper. Preheat the grill.
2 Brush with some melted butter and place under a hot grill for 3 minutes. Turn it over, brush again with melted butter and grill for a further 3 minutes.
3 Serve with new potatoes and a wedge of lemon – simple and brilliant.

Sole baked with leeks

The leeks form a bed for the sole to bake on, covered in a creamy wine sauce.

SERVES 2
25g butter
4 leeks, sliced into rings
1 small onion, very finely chopped
2 garlic cloves, chopped
125ml dry white wine
100ml double cream
2 Dover sole, cleaned and skinned on both sides
salt and pepper

1   Preheat the oven to 190°C/gas mark 5.
2   Heat the butter in a frying pan, add the leeks, onion and garlic and cook over a medium heat until the onion is translucent.
3   Add the wine and bring to the boil. Turn down the heat and stir in the cream.
4   Using a slotted spoon, spoon the leeks into an ovenproof dish and lay the fish on top. Season with salt and pepper.
5   Pour the rest of the sauce over the fish and leeks and bake for 12 minutes. Serve on its own or with new potatoes.

Sole with cheese and bacon

The amazing flavour of this dish took me by surprise because I simply didn't expect it. It came about because we started to make a lot of halloumi cheese at home (it's really easy, by the way). I dare say you can use any fish, but sole fillets wrap easily.

SERVES 4 AS A STARTER
olive oil for brushing
4 sole fillets
4 pieces of halloumi, each about 3cm long by 1cm square
4 bacon rashers – good fatty bacon is best
pepper
juice of 1 lemon

1   Preheat the oven to 180°C/gas mark 4. Brush a baking dish with olive oil.
2   Wrap a sole fillet around each piece of halloumi, then wrap a bacon rasher around the fish. Secure each parcel with a wooden cocktail stick. They shouldn't need salt – the cheese and bacon are salty enough – but a seasoning of pepper is good.
3   Bake for 25–30 minutes. Serve with a drizzle of lemon juice.

Haddock

The haddock is a coldwater fish from the North Atlantic. It has a dark smudge above the pectoral fin, and a distinctive dark lateral line with silvery sides and belly. Haddock are about 40–60cm long and usually weigh about 1–2kg each.

You can use haddock instead of cod in recipes if you like, but it does have a distinctive flavour of its own. Personally I prefer it, even though it does seem to be a little more expensive. It has a white flaky flesh which cooks well.

Haddock is often smoked. For some reason the smoked fish is often dyed bright yellow, but this is quite unnecessary and these days it's usually quite easy to find undyed smoked haddock.

Lemon haddock

This is a lovely treat to make the most of really fresh haddock.

SERVES 4
4 large haddock fillets
plain flour for dusting
25g butter
juice and zest of 1 lemon
handful of finely chopped chives
handful of finely chopped parsley
salt and pepper

1 Dust the haddock with flour.
2 Heat the butter in a frying pan over a moderate heat.
3 Add the haddock fillets, skin side up, and cook for 4 minutes.
4 Turn the fish over, add the lemon juice and baste the haddock.
   Sprinkle the chives, parsley, lemon zest, salt and pepper over the fish
   and cook for 3 minutes. Serve with mashed potato, or on pitta bread
   with salad.

Cidered haddock casserole

You can use any firm white fish for this recipe. You can also use any cheese you fancy – I like it with crumbly Wensleydale.

SERVES 4
butter for greasing
500g haddock, cod, pollack or similar white fish fillets, skinned
4 ripe tomatoes, sliced
50g closed-cup mushrooms, sliced
salt and pepper
150ml dry cider
50g fresh breadcrumbs
50g cheese, grated

1   Preheat the oven to 190°C/gas mark 5. Butter a casserole dish.
2   Cut the fish into 3cm pieces and lay them in the casserole dish.
3   Put a layer of tomatoes on top, then a layer of mushrooms. Repeat the layers until you have used all the tomatoes and mushrooms. Season with salt and pepper, then pour over the cider. Cover and cook in the oven for 20 minutes.
4   Preheat the grill. Remove the casserole lid and sprinkle over the breadcrumbs and then the cheese. Place under the hot grill for about 3 minutes until the topping is brown and bubbling. Serve with boiled new potatoes or thick chips.

Haddock fish cakes

Cod or hake may also be used, or a combination of two or three.

MAKES 4 LARGE CAKES
450g haddock, cut into large chunks
1 bay leaf
200ml milk
300g cooked potatoes, suitable for mashing
1 spring onion, white part only, finely chopped
grated zest of 1 small lemon
1 tbsp chopped fresh parsley
salt and black pepper
a little flour
1 egg, lightly beaten
100g fresh breadcrumbs
oil for shallow frying

1 Put the fish into a pan and add the bay leaf and milk. Bring to the boil, then reduce the heat and simmer for about 4 minutes. Turn off the heat, cover with a lid and leave to one side.
2 Mash the potatoes with the spring onion, lemon zest and parsley. Add 1 tablespoon of the fish cooking liquor. Season to taste.
3 Drain the fish and flake roughly. Leave to cool for 5 minutes.
4 Add the fish to the potatoes and mix well. Leave the mixture to cool completely.
5 Flour your hands lightly. Divide the fish mixture into four equal parts and form into round cakes about 2cm deep. Chill for 30 minutes.
6 Pour the egg into a shallow dish and put the breadcrumbs on a plate.
7 Heat sufficient oil in a frying pan to come about halfway up the fish cakes.
8 Dip the fish cakes into the beaten egg to coat all over, then coat them in the breadcrumbs. Fry for 4–5 minutes on each side until deep golden brown. Serve with tartare sauce and a green salad.

Garlic and anchovy-topped haddock with parsley potato cakes

I love the saltiness of anchovies combined with garlic and a touch of tomato: they go so well with the haddock. I usually find it easier to make the potato cakes first (see overleaf) and keep them warm while I prepare the fish.

SERVES 4

2 tbsp olive oil, plus extra for greasing
2 large slices of wholemeal bread
5 anchovy fillets – don't worry about draining off the oil,
    it will add to the flavour
3 garlic cloves
1 tbsp tomato purée
6 black olives
black pepper
2 tbsp chopped fresh parsley
4 haddock fillets, about 180–200g each

1   Preheat the oven to 200°C/gas mark 6 and oil a baking tray.
2   Place all the ingredients, except for the fish, in a food processor and whiz until finely chopped. Stir and whiz again.
3   Place the haddock fillets on the prepared baking sheet. Spoon a quarter of the bread and anchovy mixture on to each piece. Press down gently with your hands.
4   Bake for about 10–15 minutes until the fish is cooked and the topping golden brown. Serve with potato cakes (see overleaf).

Potato cakes

SERVES 4

450g mashed potato
100g plain flour, plus extra for dusting
50g self-raising flour
3 tbsp single cream
1 tbsp chopped fresh parsley
salt and pepper
oil for shallow frying

1   Place the potato in a mixing bowl and sift the two flours together
    into the bowl.
2   Add the cream and parsley and season to taste. Mix everything
    together with your hands.
3   Divide the mixture into four equal portions and roll each into a ball.
    Coat your hands in flour and flatten the balls to make four patties.
4   Heat the oil in a frying pan or griddle and fry the cakes for about 3
    minutes on each side. Keep the heat to medium – not too hot – so
    that the cakes cook in the centre while becoming deep golden brown
    on the outside.

Cullen skink

The village of Cullen on the north-east coast of Scotland, between Aberdeen and Inverness, is famous for its broth or *skink*, based on Finnan haddie (locally produced cold-smoked haddock) and potatoes. It is a very rich dish, definitely more than a soup. Finnan haddock is hard to come by, so use ordinary smoked haddock, ideally natural, undyed fish.

SERVES 4–6
450g smoked haddock
1 onion, roughly chopped
600ml water or fish/chicken stock
3 small leeks, sliced
220g potatoes, boiled and mashed
50g butter
1 egg yolk
300ml single cream
salt and pepper
2 tbsp chopped fresh parsley

1 Put the fish and onion in a saucepan and just cover with water. Bring slowly to the boil, then simmer gently for about 8 minutes.
2 Remove the fish from the liquid and set aside. Strain the cooking liquor into a jug or bowl; discard the onion and any bones.
3 Flake the fish, removing all the bones and skin.
4 Put the fish cooking liquor and the water or stock into a pan and bring to the boil. Add the leeks and simmer until they are tender.
5 Turn the heat down to a gentle simmer. Add the mashed potato and butter and stir in the fish.
6 Beat the egg yolk together with the cream and stir this into the soup. Season with salt and pepper and simmer very gently for 2 minutes.
7 Serve in bowls with some parsley sprinkled on top.

Omelette 'Arnold Bennett'

This delicious way of serving eggs, smoked haddock and cheese was first prepared for the novelist Arnold Bennett, in London's Savoy Grill. He would request this dish for breakfast in any hotel he stayed in thereafter. This is a slightly less complex version of the original but is still very tasty.

SERVES 2

120g Finnan haddock or any good quality undyed smoked haddock
100ml milk
2 tsp cornflour mixed with 2 tbsp cold milk
salt and pepper
1 tbsp freshly grated Parmesan cheese
1 tbsp grated Gruyère cheese
20g butter
4 eggs, beaten
2 tbsp double cream

1 Poach the fish in the milk for about 10 minutes. When cooked, lift the fish out into a bowl and flake, removing any bones and skin.
2 Heat the poaching liquid and simmer to reduce slightly. Stir in the cornflour and cook until it thickens. Season to taste. Stir in the cheeses and pour over the fish. Stir gently to mix.
3 Heat the grill to its hottest setting.
4 Melt the butter in a large frying pan and when it starts to foam, add the eggs. Cook over a medium heat until the omelette is just set but still runny on top.
5 Spoon the fish mixture over the eggs and drizzle over the cream. Place the omelette under the grill and cook until the top begins to brown and bubble. Serve immediately.

Smoked haddock pie

This my Mum's fish pie recipe, although I use a little more fish than she used to. It is topped with puff pastry and I serve it with mashed potatoes or potato croquettes and a green vegetable.

SERVES 4

25g butter
5 spring onions, finely chopped
250ml fish stock
150ml milk (you can use all milk if you have no stock)
200g smoked haddock fillet, cut into chunks
250g haddock fillet, cut into chunks
1 rounded tbsp cornflour mixed with 2 tbsp cold milk
salt and pepper
100g frozen peas or green beans, defrosted
1 tbsp chopped fresh parsley
100ml single cream
350g puff pastry

1 Preheat the oven to 190°C/gas mark 5.
2 Melt the butter in a large saucepan and fry the onions gently for a few minutes until they are soft but not browned.
3 Pour in the stock and milk and bring to the boil, then turn down to a simmer and add the fish. Poach the fish for about 5 minutes, then lift it out and put to one side.
4 Bring the liquor to the boil and whisk in the cornflour mixture, season to taste and add the peas or beans and parsley. Simmer for 2–3 minutes.
5 Stir in the cream and add the fish. Pour the filling into a deep ovenproof dish.
6 Roll out the pastry to just fit the top of the dish, resting the pastry inside the dish rather than on the sides.
7 Bake for 20–30 minutes or until the pastry is well risen and golden brown.

Hake

Buying hake can be somewhat alarming. It looks so aggressive, with its teeth sticking out, one worries about losing a finger. In fact, it is a member of the cod family, with a long narrow body, usually about 60–75cm long. Hake fillets are firm, white and tasty, and can be used instead of any other white fish, though it is somewhat more expensive. It's very popular in Spain and Portugal, where it is sometimes called the King of the Sea.

Hake poached in white wine

A simple dish that showcases the flavour of fresh hake.

SERVES 2
250ml dry white wine
150ml water
1 star anise
2 hake fillets, about 200g each
large handful of chopped parsley
salt and pepper

1 Put the wine, water and star anise into a large pan and bring to the boil.
2 Turn the heat down to a gentle simmer, add the fish and poach for about 10 minutes.
3 Remove the fish and keep warm in a low oven. Discard the star anise.
4 Add the parsley to the poaching liquid, season to taste and boil for 10 minutes to reduce the liquid until it thickens slightly.
5 Serve with the sauce spooned over the fish.

Hake with onions, potatoes and garlic

I got the idea for this recipe from Keith Floyd who cooked it
at a monastery in Galicia, north-west Spain. I had something
very similar in San Sebastián in the Basque Country. It calls
for big chunks of hake, poached and then combined with
garlic and potatoes and baked.

SERVES 4

4 thick hake steaks
3 onions: 1 chopped, 2 sliced into thin rings
750g potatoes, peeled and cut into 5mm slices
5 garlic cloves, chopped
125ml dry white wine
125ml double cream
salt and pepper

1   Preheat the oven to 160°C/gas mark 3.
2   Place the hake in a large pan of boiling water with the chopped
    onion. Reduce the heat and simmer very gently for 10 minutes.
3   Meanwhile, boil the potatoes for 5 minutes then drain and pat dry.
4   Layer the potatoes in an earthenware pot or deep baking dish and
    scatter the garlic over the top, then cover with the onion rings.
5   Place the hake steaks on top, pour over the wine and then the
    cream. Season with salt and pepper. Bake for 15 minutes or until the
    potatoes are tender when pierced with a skewer.

Variation
★   Instead of using white wine, you can use some of the fish poaching
    liquor. Indeed, you can poach the fish in milk and make an even
    creamier dish.

Halibut

The halibut is a flatfish found in the cold waters of the North Pacific and Atlantic oceans. It is one of the largest of flatfish, usually up to 1 metre long, although it can grow to more than 2 metres. It has firm white flesh and an excellent clean flavour. Like all flatfish it gives four fillets, but from larger fish the fillets can be divided into smaller portions. Halibut is also often sold sliced into steaks.

Fritto misto di mare

The name of this classic Italian dish means simply 'fried mixed seafood'. In Italy it's served with lemon quarters, nothing else, though I might add some tartare sauce and salad. Halibut is not a traditional ingredient in the Mediterranean, but the firmness of its flesh makes it ideal for quick frying. It doesn't matter what fish you include; a large selection is the best idea. It is nice to include a mixture of peeled and shell-on prawns – but don't coat the shell-on prawns with flour.

It really is best if you have a deep fat fryer for this recipe, so that you can cook the fish without it sticking together.

SERVES 6
1kg mixed fish and shellfish, such as halibut, sardines, sprats or whitebait, squid (calamari), prawns
75g plain flour
large pinch of salt
oil for deep frying

1 Clean and prepare your fish and shellfish, descaling where necessary and removing all the bones from larger fish. Cut the white fish into pieces about 4–8cm long.
2 Heat the oil to 180°C in a deep fat fryer; test by dropping a cube of bread into the oil – it should immediately sizzle and should brown within a minute.
3 Season the flour with a good pinch of salt and toss the fish in the seasoned flour, keeping the different types of fish separate.
4 You will need to cook the fish and shellfish in batches to avoid reducing the temperature of the oil too much. Fry the fish for 4–6 minutes, depending on thickness, and the calamari for 2–4 minutes. Drain on kitchen paper and keep the cooked fish warm in a low oven until you have cooked all the fish and shellfish.

Steamed halibut steaks with lemon and ginger

This simple dish seals in the flavour of the halibut. You can add a little cayenne pepper if you wish, just a light dusting over the fish.

SERVES 4
a little olive oil
16 thin slices of peeled fresh ginger
16 thin slices of lemon
4 halibut fillets, about 125g each
salt and pepper
juice of 1 lemon

1   Cut four sheets of foil large enough to make a parcel of the fish and coat the foil with olive oil. Place two slices of ginger and two slices of lemon on top.
2   Lay the fish on top of the lemon and ginger, season lightly and then place another two slices of ginger and two slices of lemon on top.
3   Drizzle the lemon juice equally over the four portions. Seal the foil parcels and steam for 10 minutes. Serve with rice.

Herring

'You shall have a fishy on a little dishy when the boat comes in'. The herring has been one of the most important fish from the North Atlantic for many hundreds of years, mainly because it is easy to preserve them by salting. Landed in vast numbers around the coast of Scotland and northern England, they were salted and either stored in barrels or smoked so they could be transported by cart to towns and cities. Long before bacon and eggs were considered to be the staple breakfast in the UK, people were eating kippers: salted and smoked herring.

The round, silver-grey fish is usually about 20–30cm long. Its flesh is richly flavoured but full of small bones, which have reduced the popularity of this fish. It's usually easy to remove the bones of a cooked fish; most of them are attached to the backbone, so get hold of the backbone at the head end and pull gently, which should lift away most of the bones.

Deep-fried herring

Deep-fried herring is _talking food_, in that you might as well have a good chat while you prise the flesh from the bones. But at the same time you might like to concentrate!

SERVES 2

4 herring, descaled, gutted, backbone and fins removed
4 tbsp plain flour
½ tsp salt
½ tsp white pepper
oil for deep frying

1 Wash the herring and allow any excess water to drip off.
2 Mix the flour, salt and pepper. Coat both inside and outside of the fish with the seasoned flour.
3 Heat the oil to 180°C in a deep fat fryer; test by dropping a cube of bread into the oil – it should immediately sizzle and and should brown within a minute. Deep fry the herring for 5 minutes or until golden brown. Drain on kitchen paper. Serve with tartare sauce or mustard mayonnaise.

Herring with oats

This is a traditional Scottish dish. Essentially it is shallow-fried herring fillets covered in an oat and egg mixture.

SERVES 2
6 herring fillets
250g rolled oats
salt and pepper
1 egg, beaten
oil for shallow frying

1 Make sure the fish is descaled and pin-boned. The more time spent removing bones the better the dish will be.
2 Season the oats with salt and pepper and mix with the egg. Coat the fillets in the oat mixture.
3 Heat the oil in a frying pan until it is very hot. Add the fillets and fry for 3 minutes on one side, then 2 minutes on the other. Serve immediately.

Kippers

There are many ways to cook kippers (whole smoked herring, split butterfly fashion). Mostly you are simply warming them through, since they are already cured and smoked. You can also warm them through on a barbecue, in a microwave, or by the fire on a fork.

In a jug
Cut the fish into two sides and remove the heads. Place them tail up in a jug and fill with boiling water, leaving the tails uncovered. Leave for 5 minutes and then drain. Serve with knobs of butter.

Frying
Simply place in a frying pan, skin side up, over a low heat and warm through. Serve with butter.

Grilling
Place the fish skin down on the grill, top with knobs of butter and grill for 3 minutes.

John Dory

This fish looks scary, like some kind of dragon fish, or something from *Stingray*, the children's TV show of the 1960s. It certainly doesn't look very edible, but it is one of the tastiest fish you could ever wish to eat, with firm, succulent flesh. It has a huge head and a thumbprint-sized dark splodge on its side, thought to be a warding-off mechanism for would-be predators. The name John Dory is shrouded in mystery, but it is also called St Peter's fish in France, Spain, Portugal and Scandinavia.

It's not on the MSC sustainable list because there is no dedicated John Dory fishery, but it is caught as bycatch in commercial fishing, and you may catch them yourself. They vary in size, sometimes growing up to 60cm long.

Baked John Dory

Eliza Acton's *Modern Cookery for Private Families* was published in 1845. It's full of practical advice and straightforward recipes, including one for baked John Dory. She suggests removing the head, and all the spiky fins. You are probably best getting your fishmonger to do this for you; ask if you can keep the head to make fish stock.

SERVES 2
2 John Dory, descaled, cleaned and the fins removed
salt and pepper
plain flour for dusting
50g butter

1 Preheat the oven to 160°C/gas mark 3.
2 Rinse the fish under cold running water and pat dry. Season the inside of the fish and dust the outside with flour.
3 Place the fish on a baking tray and dot 25g butter on the surface of each fish. Bake for 15 minutes or until the flesh is cooked through. Serve hot, pouring the buttery juices over the fish.

Tip
★ If you use one large John Dory it will take a little longer to cook; test after 20–25 minutes.

John Dory with brown shrimp

Ask your fishmonger to clean and fillet the fish, but make sure he or she gives you the head and bones to make your stock. Fish stock is very quick to make and is vastly superior to any stock cube you can buy.

SERVES 4 AS A STARTER
100g butter
100g shallots, finely chopped
4–6 garlic cloves, finely chopped
200ml fish stock
150g brown shrimp
150ml double cream
handful of parsley, chopped
1 tbsp olive oil
2 John Dory, filleted

1 Melt 50g of the butter in a saucepan, add the shallots and garlic and sweat over a low heat; do not brown.
2 Add the fish stock and bring to the boil. Reduce the heat and simmer to reduce by half. Add the shrimp to the reduced stock, together with the cream and parsley.
3 Heat the remaining butter and the oil in a frying pan over a low–medium heat. Add the fish fillets and cook gently for about 3 minutes on each side, being careful not to burn the butter. Serve the fish on warmed plates with the shrimp sauce spooned over the top.

Lemon sole

A bit of a misnomer, this, because it is not a sole and it isn't lemon either in flavour or colour. It is a common flatfish with a mottled grey-brown upper skin, and is really good eating.

Fried lemon sole

You can choose what you add to this: if you don't like capers or olives, leave them out; add chopped fresh herbs such as parsley, oregano or basil. No seasoning is needed because the olives are salty – but if you omit them you might wish to season with salt to taste.

SERVES 2
50g butter
2 spring onions, very finely chopped
1 garlic clove, crushed and chopped
4 lemon sole fillets
about 50g capers, drained
25g stoned black olives, chopped

1   Melt the butter in a frying pan over a medium heat, add the spring onions and garlic and cook for a minute or two.
2   Place the fillets in the pan, then add the capers and olives. Cook for about 4 minutes or until golden brown, basting with the flavoured butter. Serve immediately, with boiled new potatoes.

Lemon sole with anchovy and lemon crust

Lemon sole is very light, yet it goes well with strong flavours such as anchovy and lemon.

SERVES 2
4 lemon sole fillets
1 tbsp plain flour
zest of 1 lemon
10g butter or 2 tsp olive oil
2 anchovy fillets
1 tbsp very finely chopped fresh parsley
50g fresh breadcrumbs
black pepper

1   Preheat the oven to 190°C/gas mark 5.
2   Coat the fish lightly with the flour and place on an oiled baking sheet.
3   Blend the lemon zest, butter or oil and anchovies in a bowl until smooth and well combined. Stir in the parsley, breadcrumbs and pepper to taste. Spoon the mixture over the fillets and press down well with your fingers.
4   Bake for 12–15 minutes. Serve with a medley of green vegetables. I like to steam broccoli, green beans and sugar snap peas for about 5 minutes, then toss them with butter, salt and pepper.

Mackerel

Mackerel are marked with wavy black lines along their backs, with iridescent silvery sides and belly. They are members of the tuna family, and a number of different species are known by the name 'mackerel'. They are very numerous and have become a staple of many peoples around the world. Quick moving and voraciously hungry, they come inshore to breed and feed (during the summer months in the UK), and this is mainly when they are fished, by line fishermen using bright, flashing 'spinners' that attract the fish.

Being oily fish, rich in omega-3 fats, mackerel are very nutritious. I find cleaning and filleting mackerel is a messy business, as they have numerous small bones and filleting can be difficult without breaking the flesh, but thankfully they have tiny scales, which can be left on.

Classically, mackerel is served with a sharp-tasting sauce to counteract its oily richness. Sour gooseberries make the traditional sauce in England and northern France; other recipes might call for rhubarb or cranberries, or mustard.

Grilled mackerel

These simple fish are so tasty they make good eating on their own, with no additions or sauces.

1 Trim the fins, gut the fish and wash inside and out. Leave the head on. Pat dry and score the fish two or three times on each side. Brush the whole fish with a little olive oil and sprinkle with salt and pepper.
2 Cook them under a hot grill, or throw them on the barbecue. They take about 2–3 minutes on each side. Serve with lemon wedges.

Grilled mackerel with gooseberry sauce

A classic French dish; if you like gooseberries, this is heaven!

SERVES 2
25g butter
250g gooseberries
100ml double cream
4 mackerel fillets
olive oil
salt and pepper

1　Melt the butter in a heavy-bottomed saucepan and add the goose-berries. Cover and cook for 30 minutes over a very low heat, stirring occasionally and checking that the gooseberries don't burn.
2　When softened, mash the berries and then stir in the cream and heat for a few more minutes, stirring. Set aside.
3　While the gooseberries are cooking, brush the mackerel on both sides with olive oil and season with salt and pepper.
4　Preheat the grill. Place the fish on a baking sheet and grill, skin side up, for 5 minutes. Serve with the sauce.

Mackerel Dijonnaise

Baking it in the oven with wine or stock is a popular way to cook mackerel. I've modified this recipe from one I found in *Larousse Gastronomique* – the best book in the world for food lovers.

SERVES 4

1 tbsp olive oil
2 tsp butter
1 large onion, finely chopped
25g plain flour
300ml dry white wine
salt and pepper
8 mackerel fillets
1 tbsp Dijon mustard

1 Preheat the oven to 200°C/gas mark 6.
2 Heat the olive oil and butter in a saucepan, add the onion and cook gently until translucent.
3 Add the flour and stir vigorously until incorporated. Pour the wine in slowly while stirring to make sure there are no lumps. Season to taste with salt and pepper.
4 Place the mackerel in a baking dish and pour the sauce over. Bake for 15 minutes.
5 Remove the fish to warmed plates. Add the mustard to the sauce, stirring it in until completely incorporated. To serve, pour the sauce over the fish.

Baked mackerel with apple stuffing and paprika couscous

The mixture of apple and onion in the stuffing balances the full flavour of the meaty mackerel. Serve with paprika-flavoured couscous (opposite) for additional flavour.

SERVES 4

1 lemon, halved

4 mackerel, gutted

50g butter

1 small onion, finely chopped

2 apples (Granny Smith or Braeburn are the best for the tang
   and juiciness), peeled, cored and diced

100g fresh breadcrumbs

1 egg, beaten

3 tbsp plain flour seasoned with salt and pepper

1 Preheat the oven to 190°C/gas mark 5. Oil a baking sheet or shallow roasting pan.
2 Rub the lemon all over the mackerel.
3 Melt the butter in a frying pan and fry the onion gently for a few minutes without browning.
4 Add the apples and cook for 3–4 minutes. Stir in the breadcrumbs and remove from the heat.
5 Dip the fish into the beaten egg, then in the seasoned flour, and place on the oiled baking sheet.
6 Stuff each fish with a quarter of the stuffing, pushing it well into the body cavity. Bake the mackerel for about 25 minutes until the skin is golden brown. Serve with paprika couscous.

Paprika couscous

200g couscous
1 tbsp olive oil
1 small onion, finely chopped
1 garlic clove, chopped
2 tsp paprika
1 tbsp lemon juice

1 Prepare the couscous according to the packet instructions.
2 Heat the oil in a frying pan and fry the onion and garlic very gently until soft.
3 Sprinkle over the paprika and lemon juice and then stir the onion mixture into the couscous.

Variation

★ While the onion is frying, add a small chopped red pepper and some chopped mushrooms. This is particularly tasty with grilled or steamed white fish.

Monkfish

This is an ugly brute of a fish, often growing to well over a metre in length and with a huge mouth. It is also known as an anglerfish, which describes how it feeds; it has a little appendage on a modified spine over its mouth that it uses as a fishing rod, hoping to attract its prey. This fish is nearly all mouth, while the only edible part is the tail, which is what you'll find on sale, either whole or as fillets. It has a central bone that is quite easy to remove, but is covered in a tough membrane; if you are lucky the fishmonger will have taken this off to reveal the firm white flesh.

It was at one time a cheap fish, but has now more than caught up with others on the market. Monkfish is a good substitute for any white fish, for example in a curry – or cook it simply, to show off its particular characteristics.

Barbecued monkfish

The thing I like about cooking on a barbecue is you can make it up as you go along. Your marinade can be as simple as olive oil and garlic, or could include wine, citrus juice, herbs – more or less whatever you like. This recipe uses white wine, garlic and honey.

SERVES 4–6
4 garlic cloves, crushed and chopped
1 small onion, finely chopped
2 tbsp honey
75ml dry white wine
4 monkfish fillets, about 200g each

1 Mix together the garlic, onion, honey and wine. Put the fish in a bowl and cover with the marinade. Cover and leave in the fridge for at least 2 hours.
2 When you are ready to cook, preheat the barbecue. Remove the fish from the marinade and cook on the barbecue for about 10 minutes, turning regularly.

Black pepper-coated monkfish

This works well with any firm-fleshed white fish – or try it with raw prawns.

SERVES 2

½ tsp coarse sea salt
1 tsp black peppercorns
50g fresh breadcrumbs
2 monkfish fillets, about 200g each
1 tbsp milk
4 tbsp olive oil

1 Put the salt and peppercorns in a mortar and grind together until mixed but not too fine. Stir the pepper mixture into the breadcrumbs.
2 Dip the fish into the milk and press the salt and pepper mixture all over.
3 Heat the oil in a frying pan. When hot, add the fish and fry for about 3 minutes on each side until the fish is deep golden and cooked through.
4 Serve on a warmed plate, with green vegetables or salad leaves.

Ambot tik

This recipe, meaning *sour and spicy*, is from Goa, where the cuisine is influenced by centuries of Portuguese rule. The sourness traditionally comes from tamarind, and if you like you could add a little tamarind paste or a splash of vinegar to the masala paste.

SERVES 4
750g monkfish fillets
salt and pepper
2 tbsp olive oil
1 onion, finely chopped
50g peeled, chopped tomatoes

Masala paste
about 3 small red chillies (it's up to you how hot you would like it to be)
½ tsp cumin seeds
½ tsp coriander seeds
½ tsp black pepper
4 garlic cloves, chopped
1cm piece of fresh ginger, chopped
1 tbsp honey

1 First make the masala paste: put the chillies, cumin, coriander, pepper, garlic and ginger into a mortar and grind to a paste, or simply whiz them in a blender. Stir in the honey and set aside.
2 Cut the fish into bite-sized pieces and season with salt and pepper. Set aside.
3 Heat the oil in a wide pan and fry the onion and tomatoes for a few minutes.
4 Add the masala paste and stir in. Add the fish and cook over a low heat for 10–15 minutes until cooked through. Serve with rice.

Monkfish one pot

A simple and satisfying supper dish; you can use any kind of mushrooms here.

SERVES 4
2 tbsp olive oil
2 tsp butter
1 large leek, chopped
50g mushrooms, chopped
2 garlic cloves, chopped
80ml dry white wine
salt and pepper
4 monkfish fillets, about 120g each
8 small new potatoes, sliced and boiled until just tender
3–4 tbsp double cream
1 tbsp chopped fresh parsley

1 Heat the oil and butter in a wide frying pan and cook the leek, mushrooms and garlic together for 3–4 minutes.
2 Add the wine and cook for a minute. Season to taste.
3 Place the fish fillets among the vegetables and cook for 10 minutes, turning the fish after 5 minutes.
4 Add the cooked potatoes, stir in the cream and parsley and cook for 2–3 minutes. Serve immediately.

Mullet

Grey mullet and red mullet are very distant relations; both have slightly oily flesh, making them really nutritious and good to eat. Remember – oil makes flavour! Grey mullet are usually 30–50cm long, red mullet slightly smaller. They need to be thoroughly descaled and cleaned well, being careful to remove the guts without piercing them, because they are very strongly flavoured. Having said that, some people enjoy eating the liver of red mullet.

Grilled grey mullet

This is a very simple recipe; you can amend it to your heart's content. Instead of the onion, tomato and green pepper, you could use sliced boiled potatoes with some chopped cooked bacon and boiled green beans, cabbage or broccoli.

SERVES 2
4 grey mullet fillets, pin-boned
1 garlic clove, halved
1 lemon, sliced
1 red onion, roughly chopped
1 large tomato, roughly chopped
1 green pepper, deseeded and chopped
salt and pepper
about 3–4 tbsp olive oil

1   Rub the fish all over with the cut surface of the garlic and the lemon. Preheat the grill.
2   Put the chopped onion, tomato and pepper on a sheet of foil and lay it on a grill tray.
3   Arrange the fish on top of the vegetables and season with salt and pepper. Drizzle the fish and vegetables with olive oil and grill for 4–6 minutes on each side, depending on the thickness of the fillet. Serve the fish with the onion, tomato and pepper mixture.

Red mullet with tomato dressing

This is a take on a modern classic French sauce which goes well with all kinds of fish. It is simply an infusion of tomato, lemon, basil and the very best quality olive oil.

SERVES 4
4 red mullet, filleted and pin-boned
1–2 tbsp olive oil

Tomato dressing
4 large tomatoes, chopped into 5–7mm pieces
1 garlic clove, very finely sliced
125ml extra virgin olive oil
juice of 1 lemon
25g fresh basil, finely chopped
salt and pepper

1   To make the dressing, combine all the ingredients in a bowl and season to taste. You can, if you wish, gently warm the dressing in a pan, but do not boil it, it will spoil the flavour.
2   Score the skin side of the mullet fillets and fry in a little oil until they are cooked.
3   Place a couple of tablespoons of the dressing on each serving plate. Arrange the fish on top and then spoon the rest of the dressing over the fillets.

Plaice

This flatfish is easily identifiable because its grey-brown or olive green skin is covered in orange spots. It is one of the most commercially important fish today. Plaice live on the sandy sea bed, coming inshore to feed at night, which is when they can be caught by amateur fishermen on beaches with lines. However, the majority are caught by trawler. They are overfished in many waters, so look for the MSC label (a blue tick) in supermarkets – or try dab instead.

Plaice are very popular filleted and either floured and shallow fried or battered and deep fried.

Fried plaice with parsley butter

This is a lovely way to show off the delicate flavour and texture of plaice. Serve with boiled potatoes and maybe a little salad.

SERVES 4

50g butter
2 tbsp finely chopped parsley
8 plaice fillets
salt and pepper
oil for shallow frying
juice of 1 lemon

1 Melt the butter in a saucepan over a low heat and stir in the parsley.
2 Season the fish and fry the fillets in a little oil for about 3–4 minutes on each side.
3 Pour the lemon juice over the fish and then spoon over the parsley butter to serve.

Plaice fingers

If you wanted to be fancy, you could call these goujons. Either way, they are great finger food.

SERVES 4
8 plaice fillets
plain flour for dusting
salt and pepper
bowl of milk
oil for deep frying

1 Cut the fillets into large finger-sized pieces. Season the flour.
2 Dip the fingers of fish into the milk and then into the flour; dust off the excess flour, or it will fall into the hot oil and taint it.
3 Heat the oil to 180°C in a deep fat fryer; test by dropping a cube of bread into the oil – it should immediately sizzle and should brown within a minute. Fry the fish in batches until golden brown, drain on kitchen paper and serve with tartare sauce and lemon wedges.

Sardines

This is the most important food fish in the world: oily, tasty and abundant. Bigger than a handbreadth they are sometimes called pilchards, but are the same fish. They need to be descaled and gutted, but the bones are soft, and good cooking renders them generally edible. Even the backbone of smaller sardines can be eaten; it's a matter of personal taste. If you want to remove the backbone, run the filleting knife along both sides of the backbone to make a shallow V shape and pull out the bone.

Grilled sardines with tomato and basil

Inspired by an Italian dish, this mix of oily fish, tomato, olive oil and crusty bread is amazing!

SERVES 4
2 tbsp olive oil
1 red onion, finely chopped
2 garlic cloves, chopped
1 tbsp chopped fresh basil
350g fresh tomatoes, finely chopped
750g sardines, cleaned

1 Heat the oil in a saucepan, add the onion, garlic and basil and cook over a low heat until the onion is translucent. Add the tomatoes and remove from the heat.
2 Grill the sardines until cooked through, about 3 minutes on each side.
3 Arrange the fish on a warmed serving dish and pour the tomato sauce over them. Serve immediately with warm crusty bread such as ciabatta.

Sea bass

This is a lovely fish with a mild, almost nutty flavour. It's easy to cook and very popular. So popular, in fact, that it has become threatened, and a moratorium on fishing this species is in place at the time of writing. Fishing is banned between January and June; and from July to December the catch is limited. Recreational fishers are allowed one bass a day. Until stocks of wild sea bass recover, you should choose farmed bass if you want to try the recipes on the following pages.

Fried sea bass with mustard mayo

This simple dish can be completed in a few minutes and makes a great midweek treat.

SERVES 2

4 tbsp mayonnaise
1 tsp English mustard
4 sea bass fillets, skin on
salt and pepper
1 tbsp butter
1 tbsp light oil

1 Mix the mayo and mustard and set aside.
2 Lightly season the fillets on both sides.
3 Heat the butter and oil in a frying pan over a moderate heat. Add the fillets, skin side down, and cook for 6 minutes, then turn and cook for about 4 minutes on the other side.
4 Serve with the mustard mayo, and with a rocket salad.

Sea bass with rocket and butter sauce

Peppery rocket is delicious with subtly flavoured firm fish.
Boiled new potatoes or mashed Maris Pipers go well with this.

SERVES 2
2 sea bass fillets
salt and pepper
2–3 tbsp olive or sunflower oil

Rocket and butter sauce
50g butter
3 shallots, finely chopped
3 anchovies
250ml vegetable or fish stock
200g rocket leaves, roughly chopped
50ml double cream

1　To make the sauce, melt the butter in a small saucepan and add the shallots and anchovies. Stir until the anchovies have melted and the shallots have softened.
2　Add the stock and bring to the boil. Reduce the heat to a simmer, then add the rocket and simmer for 2–3 minutes.
3　Whiz in a blender or use a hand blender. Stir in the cream. Leave to one side while you cook the fish.
4　Season the fish with a little salt and pepper.
5　Heat the oil in a frying pan and fry the fish gently for 2–3 minutes on each side.
6　Reheat the sauce in the pan. Place the fish on warmed plates and serve with the sauce.

Shad

This is a large, herring-like fish which spawns up rivers, and can be caught inland and at sea. There are various species of shad worldwide, caught in Scandinavia, Scotland and North America; it is now quite rare in Western Europe. It is a rather bony fish and therefore has to be treated very carefully. Wash the outside of the fish in plenty of running water to remove the mud from between the scales. Gut carefully and wash the inside with plenty of salty water, being sure to remove all traces of blood. Fillet in the normal way, taking extra care when pin-boning the fillet.

Once you have bought or caught a shad, make sure you use it as quickly as possible, as they don't take to lying around too long. Leave the fillet in milk for a couple of hours before cooking, which keeps the smell down.

Fried shad

This makes good finger food or a snack at a barbecue party. It looks super served in paper cones with a wedge of lemon.

SERVES 4
4 shad fillets
milk for soaking
3–4 tbsp plain flour
salt and pepper
oil for deep frying

1 Soak the fillets in milk for a couple of hours.
2 Drain and cut each fillet into 5cm pieces and pat dry. Season the flour with salt and pepper.
3 Heat the oil to 180°C in a deep fat fryer; test by dropping a cube of bread into the oil – it should immediately sizzle and should brown within a minute.
4 Dust the fish with the seasoned flour and place in the hot oil. Cook for 5 minutes or until the fish is a good golden colour. Drain on kitchen paper and serve with lemon wedges.

Skate

The common skate is one of the largest creatures found in British waters: they can live for more than 60 years and grow to more than 2.5 metres across their wingspan. Sadly they are no longer common, but are now a critically endangered species. However, the fish sold by fishmongers and supermarkets as 'skate' may come from various types of ray. Only the 'wings' are sold as food, and they are not only tasty but also bone free, having cartilage from which it is easy to lift the flesh once cooked.

Baked skate

This simple dish might be easy, but it is really the best way of cooking skate in my view.

SERVES 2
2 tbsp olive oil
2 skate wings, about 350g each
salt and pepper
250g plum tomatoes, chopped
150ml dry white wine

1 Preheat the oven to 200°C/gas mark 6.
2 Add the oil to a large baking dish. Season the skate with salt and pepper, place in the dish and bake for 15 minutes.
3 Add the tomatoes and wine and bake for a further 10 minutes.
4 Check that the fish is cooked: the flesh should lift away easily. Taste the sauce and adjust the seasoning to taste. Serve with wedges of lemon and buttered boiled new potatoes.

Skate with beurre noisette and nasturtiums

Beurre noisette, or brown butter sauce, is a classic with skate and other meaty flatfish, such as halibut. This is a beautiful dish to make if you grow nasturtiums. If not, it is traditionally made with capers (rinse to remove some of the vinegar and pat dry) and a squeeze of lemon juice at the end.

SERVES 4
125g butter
3 tbsp nasturtium fruits, chopped
small handful of chopped fresh parsley
4 skate wings
salt
a few nasturtium flowers

1   To make the sauce, heat the butter slowly in a saucepan until it just starts to brown, stirring all the time. Add the nasturtium fruits and parsley and stir in.
2   Place the fish in a large pan of salted water and bring to the boil, then reduce the heat and simmer for 10 minutes.
3   Serve the fish on warmed plates with the butter sauce spooned over and garnish with the flowers.

Tuna

These fish have been used by mankind for thousands of years; there is evidence that they were enjoyed around the Mediterranean by the ancient Egyptians, Greeks and Phoenicians. Tuna fishing on an industrial scale is a twentieth-century development which has become so competitive that many catches have inadvertently included other animals such as porpoise and dolphin. In an effort to protect dolphins, different fishing techniques have been adopted and mean that some tuna is sold as 'dolphin friendly'.

There are various species of tuna – large, strong fish that can travel at great speed for extended periods. Their meat is flavoursome, oily and very nutritious. One of the simplest ways to cook it is to marinate it in olive oil and herbs for an hour or two, then grill, barbecue or fry it.

Tuna steaks with Italian-style red sauce

This sauce is inspired by the Italian *salsa rossa*, which can be served with fish, pork or beef steaks and is also brilliant with sausages. You can prepare the sauce in advance and store it in the fridge, then simply reheat it before pouring it over the tuna.

SERVES 2

2 fresh tuna steaks
1 tbsp light olive oil
1 tbsp white wine vinegar
black pepper

Red sauce

1 large or 2 small red peppers, cut in half and deseeded
300g fresh plum tomatoes
1 small red onion, chopped
a little oil for roasting
½ tsp dried chilli flakes or 1 fresh red chilli
2 garlic cloves
1 tsp sugar
12 black olives
2 tbsp water
1 tbsp olive oil
1 tbsp white wine vinegar
handful of basil leaves, torn

1 Preheat the oven to 200°C/gas mark 6.
2 Place the tuna on a plate. Mix the oil, vinegar and black pepper and pour or brush over the steaks, making sure it coats them all over. Leave to one side.
3 To make the sauce, put the red pepper, tomatoes and onion in a roasting pan and drizzle with oil. Roast for about 15–20 minutes or until they have begun to brown.
4 Transfer the pepper, tomatoes and onion to a food processor, add the chilli, garlic, sugar, olives, water, oil and vinegar. Whiz to form a purée, then pour into a saucepan. Bring slowly to the boil while you cook the tuna.
5 Heat a griddle or frying pan and cook the tuna for 2–3 minutes on each side or until just cooked.
6 When the sauce has come to the boil, reduce the heat and simmer for 2 minutes. Add the torn basil leaves, pour the sauce over the tuna and cook together for about 3 minutes. Serve with salad.

Tuna pie

Using canned tuna, this is a thrifty but tasty recipe. I like to serve this with a salad of tomatoes and finely chopped onion.

SERVES 4

2 tbsp olive oil
1 small onion, chopped
2 garlic cloves, chopped
1 red pepper, chopped
3 potatoes (approx. 450g), cubed
salt and pepper
300ml passata
½ tsp dried oregano
1 tsp paprika
185g can tuna steak in spring water, drained and flaked
450g shortcrust pastry

1 Preheat the oven to 190°C/gas mark 5. Grease a deep pie dish.
2 Heat the oil in a large frying pan and and add the onion, garlic and red pepper and fry for about 3 minutes.
3 Stir in the potatoes and fry, stirring occasionally, for about 6 minutes until the onion is soft and the potatoes begin to colour.
4 Add salt and pepper to taste and stir in the passata, oregano and paprika. Bring to the boil, then turn down to a simmer and add the tuna. Simmer for 2–3 minutes before turning off the heat.
5 Roll out two thirds of the pastry and line the pie dish. Spoon the tuna mixture into the dish.
6 Roll out the remaining pastry for the lid. Moisten the edges of the pastry in the dish. Place the lid on the pie and crimp the edges. Make slits in the top to allow the steam to escape. Bake for about 40 minutes until the pastry is golden brown.

Turbot

This is a big flatfish, usually 40–50cm long and weighing around 2kg, although bigger fish are sometimes found. It is quite expensive and a real treat. It is a delicately flavoured fish that will give you four large fillets, but everyone seems to want to bake or poach the turbot whole – for which you'll need a big pan! As with all flatfish, gentle and simple cooking is important.

Turbot with mushrooms

The French make this with morel mushrooms, but I use whatever mushrooms are in the shops, or chopped wine caps we grow on hen-manured straw in the garden.

You can ask the fishmonger to clean and fillet the turbot – but be sure to ask for the head and bones to make a fish stock. At home you can cut the fillets into smaller pieces.

SERVES 6
500g mushrooms
2–3 tbsp olive oil
2–3 tbsp butter
salt and pepper
200ml double cream
3 shallots, very finely chopped
1.5–2kg turbot, cleaned, filleted and cut into pieces of around 125g

1 Preheat the oven to 180°C/gas mark 4.
2 If your mushrooms are large, chop them into 2cm pieces and cook gently in a mixture of oil and butter. Season to taste and add the cream. Simmer for 5 minutes then set aside.
3 Add a little oil and butter to a frying pan and cook the turbot for 3 minutes on each side.
4 Transfer the fish to a baking dish. Pour the mushrooms and cream over the top and bake for 10 minutes. Serve with boiled new potatoes.

Baked turbot with leeks and cream

Ask the fishmonger to clean the fish and cut off the fins.

SERVES 4

1 whole turbot, weighing around 1.5kg
30g butter
2 leeks, finely chopped
½ tsp dried thyme or 1 tsp fresh thyme leaves
50ml dry white wine
salt and pepper
50ml double cream
1 tbsp melted butter

1 Preheat the oven to 200°C/gas mark 6. Turbot has a rough, lumpy skin, and I often scrape off some of the bumps. Rinse the fish and dry it well.
2 Melt the butter in a pan and gently fry the leeks with the thyme until tender. Add the wine, season to taste and simmer gently for 3 minutes. Stir in the cream and remove from the heat.
3 Place the fish in a roasting pan and spoon the leeks into the cavity of the fish. Pour any remaining liquor and leeks over the fish.
4 Pour the melted butter over the fish, season with a little more salt and pepper and place in the oven for 30–40 minutes.
5 To check if the fish is cooked, cut into the flesh near the backbone and lift the flesh a little: it should be white all through. Serve with boiled new potatoes.

CHAPTER 5

Freshwater fish

It is widely thought river fish are muddy in flavour, and this might be true in certain circumstances, for some fish. Dorothy Hartley, in her book *Food in England*, makes a distinction between fish from clear-flowing rivers, brooks and mountain lakes, and 'muddy-bottom' fish. She says that muddy-bottom fish have special interlocking scales which keep the mud out when the fish is swimming against the current, but when it is still or going with the current these scales open and mud gets between them. To avoid a muddy flavour, she recommends this technique: smooth a covering of clay or salt paste over the fish from head to tail and then roast the fish whole without disturbing it. The covering is then removed along with the skin, leaving clean-tasting flesh.

Running-water fish commonly eaten include:

★ Salmon
★ Trout
★ Carp
★ Char

Muddy or still-water fish commonly eaten include:

★ Pike
★ Perch
★ Eel

Another way to avoid muddy flavours is to keep the fish alive in clean water, and then kill it just before cooking. Most people will find this rather too gruesome, and simply buying the fish from the fishmonger will suffice.

The recipes for river fish are more or less interchangeable and can be adapted for any fish you happen to catch.

Arctic char

A relative of the salmon, this fish is seen around the shores of Scandinavia and in the North Sea, but is mostly caught in the rivers and lakes where it spawns. Sometimes known as charr, it used to be a speciality in the Lake District. Often preferred to salmon because of its cleaner, firmer texture and milder flavour, this fish is a real favourite in Norway and Sweden, the Baltic states and Russia. It is now farmed, and you can tell the farmed fish by its uniform pink colour over the more variable colour of the wild type.

Arctic char with mushrooms

I modified this recipe from one I found on the internet, which seemed to be a little over-complicated. Char goes really well with mushrooms, as does most fish.

SERVES 4
4 char fillets, 150–180g each, descaled, skin left on
salt and pepper
light oil for frying
2 shallots, finely chopped
25g butter
100g chopped fresh tomatoes
handful of parsley, chopped
juice of 1 lemon
4 large Portobello mushrooms
extra virgin olive oil to serve

1   Wash the char and season both sides with salt and pepper. Set aside.
2   Heat a little oil in a saucepan and cook the shallots until translucent. Add the butter and tomatoes and bring to the boil, then immediately turn the heat to low and simmer for a few minutes. Stir in the parsley and lemon juice and season to taste.
3   Preheat the grill to moderate, then place the mushrooms under the grill for 3–4 minutes until tender.
4   Heat a little oil in a frying pan and fry the fish, skin side down, for 4 minutes, then turn and cook the other side for 3 minutes. You are looking for a really crispy skin.
5   To assemble the dish, lay a mushroom on each plate, spoon in the tomato and parsley mixture and lay the fish on top, skin side up. Drizzle with a little olive oil and scatter the remaining tomato and parsley mixture around the plate.

Arctic char with pancetta

Fish with a kick: a hot salsa is poured over the fish as it bakes in the oven. Be careful: this is a hot one!

You need two types of pancetta: long thin slices and lardons. You can use streaky bacon instead of the pancetta slices. We make our own pancetta from belly pork, and when slicing it, I get so scared of the bacon slicer that I always leave about 1cm at the end, which I chop into lardons.

SERVES 4

4 char fillets, skinned
8 slices of pancetta
2 tbsp olive oil
1 aubergine, chopped
1 red onion, chopped
1 hot chilli, chopped
3 garlic cloves, chopped
150ml dry white wine
300g chopped fresh tomatoes
6–10 olives, chopped
25g capers
handful of basil leaves, chopped
salt and pepper
100g pancetta lardons

1 Preheat the oven to 180°C/gas mark 4.
2 Wrap each fish fillet in two slices of pancetta and place in an ovenproof dish.
3 Heat the oil in a frying pan over a low heat, add the aubergine, onion, chilli and garlic and sweat until translucent.
4 Add the wine, tomatoes, olives, capers and basil and simmer gently for a few minutes. Season to taste.
5 Pour over the fish, cover with foil and bake for 40–45 minutes.

Check the liquid level from time to time; don't let it dry up – add a little more wine if needed.

6 While the fish is cooking, fry the pancetta lardons over a low heat until the fat is crispy.

7 To serve, lay a piece of fish on each plate and spoon over the remaining sauce. Top with a sprinkling of lardons.

Carp

Carp is very popular around the world, from the Far East to North America. It is a favourite in Chinese cooking as well as in Europe and lends itself to all kinds of flavours. It can have a slight muddy flavour during the summer, less so in winter. You are best buying from Chinese supermarkets, where they are sometimes kept in fresh, clean water.

Often referred to as strongly flavoured, the fish is improved by soaking in a mixture of half vinegar, half water for 30 minutes. After this time give it a good wash under cold running water. Carp is best cooked quickly, certainly never overcooked. It is ready when opaque but still moist.

Baked stuffed carp

Based on an average-sized carp, this recipe serves two, but it's easy to increase the quantities if you want to bake two or more fish.

SERVES 2
1 carp, approx. 500–750g, descaled and cleaned
300ml cold water
300ml white wine vinegar

Stuffing
1 tbsp olive oil
40g butter
1 onion, finely chopped
1 garlic clove, crushed and finely chopped
75g fresh breadcrumbs
25ml dry white wine
handful of parsley, finely chopped
25ml double cream
salt and pepper

1 Put the fish into a dish just large enough to hold it. Add the water and vinegar and leave to soak for 30 minutes.
2 While it is soaking, prepare your stuffing. Heat the oil and a tablespoon of the butter in a pan, add the onion and garlic and cook gently until softened. Add the breadcrumbs, the remaining butter and the wine and cook for 5 minutes over a low heat, stirring well. Add the parsley and stir in the cream, mixing well. Season to taste.
3 Preheat the oven to 180°C/gas mark 4.
4 Wash the soaked fish under cold running water, pat dry and season inside and out. Stuff the cavity and bake for about 45 minutes.

Chinese carp

I've experimented with various recipes to come up with this one. The fish is marinated overnight in the fridge.

SERVES 4
1kg filleted carp, cut into 7–8cm pieces
300ml cold water
300ml white wine vinegar
1 onion, sliced into rings
olive oil for brushing

Marinade
1 onion, finely chopped
4 garlic cloves
150ml soy sauce
150ml water
1 tsp five spice powder
50g dark brown sugar
1 tsp grated fresh ginger
½ tsp each of salt and black pepper

1 Put the fish pieces into a dish just large enough to hold them. Add the water and vinegar and leave to soak for 30 minutes.
2 For the marinade, put the onion, garlic, soy sauce, water, five spice, sugar, ginger, salt and pepper in a pan and bring to to the boil, stirring occasionally to dissolve the sugar. Leave to cool.
3 Layer the onion rings in a glass bowl. Wash the soaked fish under cold running water, pat dry and place on top of the onion rings. Pour the marinade over the fish, cover and leave in the fridge overnight.
4 Preheat the grill. Remove the fish from the marinade and thread on to skewers. Brush with a little olive oil and grill for 3 minutes each side. Serve with rice.

Crayfish

The ecology of the rivers of the UK, and many other parts of Europe, is such that invasive species have dislodged the natives. In many parts of Britain, the American signal crayfish is causing so much devastation to our native species that it really should be eaten. If you know where to find them (ask local fishermen) you can trap your own crayfish, but you do need permission from the government and from the landowner. The application is free, which shows the importance of getting rid of them.

Crayfish are readily available online, and from certain outlets. Buying them from a reputable supplier will mean they have already been cleaned, ready for cooking.

PREPARING AND COOKING CRAYFISH

★ If you have trapped your own crayfish, they need to be purified, to allow the gut contents time to be digested. Leave them in a bucket of fresh water for 24 hours.

★ Crayfish are really sweet 'little lobsters' that can be killed very quickly in boiling water, so there are no real animal welfare issues with cooking them, so long as you only boil a few at a time. Usually I leave them in the freezer for about an hour first, to give them a chance to settle down. Plunge them into salted water at a rolling boil and they are dispatched within seconds.

★ You get a variety of crayfish sizes: the large ones are about 10–12cm, the small ones about 7cm. Larger ones need to be boiled for a good 5 minutes, the smaller ones about $3\frac{1}{2}$ minutes.

★ Once they are cooked, transfer to iced water to stop the cooking process, otherwise the thick shell will retain heat and continue cooking them.

★ To get the meat out, turn the crayfish onto its back and pull off the fan tail. Then pull off the lower portion from the large head end and remove the claws.

★ The head end has little meat and I usually discard it because there are guts and other organs in there I am not happy about eating, but that's just me. Some people love the rich flavour of the meat found in the upper carapace.

★ With a pair of scissors, make a cut in the outer shell of the bottom portion and twist off the shell, leaving you with the meat. Similarly, cut open the claws and remove the meat.
★ Any pieces of shell can be boiled to make stock or a sauce.

Of course, crayfish will be a good substitute for any lobster, langoustine or prawn dish, but my favourite (and the traditional) way to eat them is simply grilled on buttered toast, with a light seasoning of salt and a dusting of cayenne pepper. Glorious.

Eel

I would say from the outset that eels are best bought from your fishmonger, partly because the wild population has decreased by 95 per cent in recent years; though you can now get farmed ones. Also, it distresses me, as well as the fish, to suffer my unpractised killing technique. It is a good idea to get the fishmonger to kill, clean, skin and fillet them, otherwise you might find them too distressing a meal altogether. They are notoriously difficult to dispatch, they wriggle about long after death, and even with the heads removed can still appear to be alive. Usually the fishmonger will cool the animal in iced water or put the eel in the freezer before killing it, in much the same way as we do with lobster.

It was often said, because they are so wriggly even when dead, that the fish was skinned alive. If it is very fresh, the eel will still be wriggling when being filleted, even though it is actually dead, so it is probably best to ask your fishmonger to do the job for you.

Eels are high in fat and are very rich in vitamins A and D, so much so that eel is just as good as cod liver oil, which most children of my generation had to endure daily in large spoonfuls. An eel is much more appetising. Some people find eel too fatty, but the fat is easily removed by grilling. When making a pie, you can remove some of the fattiness by soaking the eel in vinegar for a couple of hours, then rinsing under cold running water.

In London there are still some pie and mash shops where you can buy the original fast food: eel pie and jellied eels.

Grilled eel fillets

A simple and very tasty way to cook eel. If you prefer, you can remove the skin before cooking. Make sure you use ripe, well flavoured tomatoes for the topping.

SERVES 2
4 eel fillets, about 100–150g each

Topping
1 tbsp butter for frying
2 shallots, very finely chopped
2 garlic cloves, chopped
a few capers
6 tomatoes, finely chopped
salt and pepper

1   Preheat the grill to hot.
2   To prepare the topping, heat the butter in a small pan and fry the shallots and garlic until softened. Add the capers and tomatoes and cook over a low heat for a few minutes. Season to taste.
3   Grill the eel for about 3½ minutes on each side, skin down first.
4   When cooked, lay on a plate lined with kitchen paper to absorb any excess fat, then serve on warmed plates and spoon the topping over the fish.

Ann Peckham's stewed eels

In her book, *The Complete English Cook*, first published in 1767, Ann Peckham gave a recipe for stewed eel, which I've transcribed for the modern kitchen.

SERVES 4

1kg eel fillets, skinned
butter for cooking
1 tbsp plain flour
150ml fish stock
1 onion, finely chopped
3 anchovy fillets, chopped
1 tsp grated fresh horseradish or 1 tsp horseradish sauce
150ml red wine
a little grated mace
salt and pepper

1   Cut the eel fillets into 5–7cm pieces. Fry them in a little butter until golden all over. Set aside to rest while you begin the stew.
2   Add a tablespoon of butter to a hot, heavy-bottomed pan, then add the flour and make a roux by stirring it constantly with a wooden spoon. Slowly add the stock, stirring all the time, then the onion, anchovies and horseradish. Bring to a rolling boil and add the wine.
3   Add the eel and cook over a low heat for 5 minutes.
4   Remove the eel pieces to a serving dish and strain the liquid over the fish.

Eel pie

At one time this was an inexpensive dish, but the scarcity of eel makes it rather less so today.

SERVES 4
1.5kg eel, cleaned
1 carrot, roughly chopped
1 small onion, quartered
3 garlic cloves, peeled
salt and pepper
handful of chopped parsley
150ml double cream
150g Cheddar cheese, grated
200g shortcrust pastry
1 egg, beaten (optional)

1 Place the eel into a large pan with the carrot, onion and garlic, and a little salt and pepper, cover with water and bring to the boil. Reduce the heat to a simmer and cook for 25 minutes.
2 Using a slotted spoon, remove the eel and leave until cool enough to remove the skin, and then pull the meat off the bones and place in a ceramic pie dish.
3 Preheat the oven to 190°C/gas mark 5.
4 Strain the cooking liquor. Return the liquor to a pan and heat gently until reduced by half. Remove from the heat and whisk in the cream, then stir in the cheese. Taste and check the seasoning.
5 Pour the creamy liquor over the fish, folding in gently with a fork.
6 Roll out the pastry and use to cover the pie with a lid; make a steam hole in the centre. If you wish you can glaze your pastry with beaten egg. Bake for 25 minutes. Serve with mashed potatoes or a big plateful of cabbage.

Jellied eels

Eels were once very inexpensive and were widely used to make pies and jellied eels. Jellied eels are still a popular dish in the East End of London.

SERVES 4–6
1kg eel, cleaned, skinned and boned
1 onion, finely chopped
handful of parsley, roughly chopped
about 750ml fish stock
3 sheets of gelatine
juice of 1 lemon
salt and pepper

1 Cut the eel into 10cm strips, then roll them up; hold them in position using wooden cocktail sticks, or tie some kitchen string around them.
2 Place the eel in a pan with the onion and parsley, cover with stock and bring to the boil. Reduce the heat to a simmer and cook for an hour.
3 Soak the gelatine in a little cold water.
4 Using a slotted spoon, remove the eel to a bowl. Remove the cocktail sticks or string.
5 Strain the stock and add the drained soaked gelatine; stir to dissolve, then add the lemon juice and season to taste. Pour the liquid over the fish and leave to cool: the gelatine should set.

Perch

Perch is the terror of the river: hunting in packs, like little demons, they eat anything they can get their teeth into – which is why they are so easy to catch. I doubt many fishmongers will ever have them, but amateur fishermen will have caught this animal on an almost daily basis. They were nearly wiped out a couple of decades ago by a virus, which seems not to be a problem these days.

They are said to be bony, but their flesh is such that they can be deboned really easily. They are eaten as fillets, and each fillet makes a few small mouthfuls of firm white flesh. The fish needs to be about 200g as a minimum to make it worth eating.

Floured and fried perch

This seems to be the archetypal way to cook any fish fillets. Coated in seasoned flour and fried, they take only a couple of minutes to cook, and are quite delicious.

SERVES 4
about 16 perch fillets, deboned and cleaned
125g plain flour
1 tsp salt
generous grating of black pepper
2–3 tbsp butter
1 lemon, sliced

1 Wash the fillets and pat dry.
2 Combine the flour with the salt and pepper and mix well.
3 Heat the butter in a frying pan over a moderate heat and add the lemon slices, pressing them down to squeeze out the juice.
4 Dip the fish in the flour to coat on both sides, and fry in the lemony butter.

Pike

The pike, like its cousin the zander (often called pike-perch), is a voracious carnivore. Zander is actually a kind of perch, but it resembles pike in size and habit. Pike are long, powerful fish, living for up to twenty years and growing up to 1.5 metres long, although the best pike for eating are considerably smaller. The business end is dangerously supplied with teeth, allowing it to catch and eat very large fish. If you catch your own you need a good butcher's glove just in case it gets you.

Pike has long been a welcome addition to the diet in many European countries.

CLEANING AND FILLETING PIKE
Follow the processes described in chapter 2, but the following tips may help.

★ When descaling, the scales can be helped on their way with a rinse of boiling water. You need a good grip of the tail to force the scales away.
★ Once you have cleaned the fish, the head might need some work to remove. Use a sharp, heavy knife to make a cut behind the head and then break the backbone. You might need a rolling pin to hit the back of the knife.
★ When filleting, you will find a row of V-shaped bones running parallel to the backbone. To remove these, make a V-shaped slit on both sides and lift out the bones; a little of the meat will be attached to the bones and you can use this for stock.

Baked pike fillets

Pike flesh is slightly yellow when raw, but turns white when cooked, and this is a good guide to it being ready. You should also test that the flesh flakes easily with a fork.

SERVES 4

1kg pike fillets, skinned and divided into four equal portions
salt and pepper
1 onion, sliced in rings
2 garlic cloves, sliced into slivers
200ml milk
150g grated cheese

1 Preheat the oven to 180°C/gas mark 4.
2 Season the fish well and place in an ovenproof dish.
3 Cover the fish with a layer of onion and garlic, then pour in the milk.
4 Bake for 20 minutes or until the flesh has changed colour and flakes easily. Sprinkle the cheese over the top and bake for a further 10 minutes to melt the cheese.

Pike gratin

This is one of my favourite ways to eat almost any fish, and it works particularly well with pike.

SERVES 4

2 tbsp butter
1 large onion, finely chopped
2–3 garlic cloves, finely chopped
500g fresh tomatoes, chopped
5 or 6 basil leaves, each torn into three
salt and pepper
1kg pike fillets, skinned
100g fresh breadcrumbs
50g Parmesan cheese, finely grated

1 Preheat the oven to 180°C/gas mark 4.
2 In a heavy-bottomed ovenproof pan that will also fit under your grill, heat half the butter and sweat the onion and garlic over a low heat.
3 Add the tomatoes and cook for a few minutes before adding the basil. Mix well and season to taste.
4 Cut the fish into 5cm pieces and arrange on the tomato mixture.
5 Cut the remaining butter into small cubes and dot over the fish. Cover the pan with a lid and cook in the oven for 25 minutes.
6 Preheat the grill to moderate.
7 Mix the breadcrumbs with the cheese and then liberally sprinkle over the fish. Place under the grill for 3 minutes or until the cheese and breadcrumb mixture is golden brown.

Salmon

The king of fish, when farmed, is very cheap to buy. Catching your own, however, unless you wish to run the gauntlet of the law, is very expensive indeed. Whichever way you obtain your salmon, I think it is at its best simply gutted and cooked whole: poached or roasted/baked. Either method allows you to add as much extra flavour as you like. The flesh, being oily, cooks well and there are so many tremendous recipes for salmon, it is in danger of becoming a victim of its own success.

Salmon are oceanic fish that begin life in rivers, then journey to the sea; it takes many years until they become adult, and they eventually return to their native river to spawn. Huge fish of around 30kg are occasionally found in Scandinavia. Pollution, the damming of rivers and overfishing made salmon a rare fish for a while, but stocks are increasing. Without farming, however, one would fear for its future.

My childhood Sundays were nourished almost exclusively, in summertime at least, by salmon salads. Tinned fish from Canada, liberally doused in vinegar and mashed, with a little pepper. It was many years before I realised salmon didn't just come in a tin!

In recent decades, smoked salmon has usurped canned salmon as an everyday luxury. Its distinctive flavour means that a little goes a long way, and it's a very versatile ingredient.

Roast salmon fillets

This recipe uses dill, always a great herb to go with salmon. Two large fillets are sandwiched together and wrapped in baking parchment, which keeps them moist and tender.

SERVES 6

2 large salmon fillets, each about 750g–1kg, descaled
salt and pepper
1 leek, separated into individual leaves
300g cherry tomatoes, chopped
3 shallots, finely chopped
juice of 1 lemon
handful of dill, finely chopped
1 tbsp tomato purée
100g butter, cut into small cubes
150ml dry white wine

1 Preheat the oven to 180°C/gas mark 4.
2 Wash the salmon fillets and season both sides.
3 Place a large piece of baking parchment into a large roasting pan. Cut long pieces of leek leaf into strips and place on the baking parchment. You will use this to tie the fish, so you want three or four strips, laid like train tracks.
4 Lay your first fillet on the leek strips.
5 Combine the tomatoes, shallots, lemon juice and dill and mix with the tomato purée, then roughly mix in the butter. Spoon this mixture evenly on to the first fillet, and place the second fillet on top.
6 Carefully draw the leek strips around the fillets and, taking your time, tie them to hold the 'sandwich' together.
7 Pour over the wine and then draw the baking parchment around to enclose the whole thing.
8 Bake for 40–45 minutes. Check that the fish is cooked: it should flake easily at the gentle touch of a thin knife. Serve with couscous.

Roast whole salmon

An impressive dish for a special lunch.

SERVES 6
1.5–2kg whole salmon, cleaned and descaled
2 lemons
750g fresh tomatoes, chopped
3–4 shallots, finely chopped
large handful of parsley, finely chopped
2 large potatoes, peeled and sliced into thin ovals
salt and pepper
100g butter, cut into small cubes
150ml dry white wine

1   Preheat the oven to 180°C/gas mark 4.
2   Wash the salmon inside and out. Slice one lemon in half and use this
    to squeeze and rub inside the cavity. Combine the tomatoes, shallots
    and parsley and use this mixture to stuff the cavity.
3   Line the bottom of a roasting pan with the potatoes and place the
    salmon on top. Season with salt and pepper.
4   Slice the remaining lemon and lay over the top of the salmon. Dot
    the butter over the salmon and add the wine.
5   Cover with foil and bake for 20 minutes, to allow the butter to
    permeate the flesh without burning. Remove the foil and continue
    baking for a further 20–25 minutes or so, checking that the liquid in
    the roasting pan does not dry out and adding extra wine if necessary.
6   Check the thickest part of the salmon with a thin knife; the fish
    is cooked if it flakes easily. Use a large palette knife to transfer
    the whole fish and the potatoes to a large serving dish. Serve with
    vegetables and a spoonful or two of the tomato stuffing.

Variation

★ To make an excellent sauce you can deglaze the roasting pan with a splash more wine and some cream, then whisk in some butter and season to taste.

★ You can do away with the potato bed and instead wrap the salmon in baking parchment, in which case you can simply roll the cooked salmon on to the serving dish.

Salmon with clams and mustard

This is inspired by a Spanish dish. A sprinkling of sweet paprika over the finished dish looks good and adds extra aroma.

SERVES 2

1 tbsp olive oil
1 large onion, finely chopped
3 garlic cloves, finely chopped
2 salmon fillets
300g clams in their shells, well scrubbed
125ml dry white wine
50ml fish stock
handful of chopped parsley
1 tbsp Dijon mustard
salt and pepper
1 tsp sweet paprika (optional)

1 Heat the oil in a frying pan, add the onion and garlic and cook over a moderate heat until translucent – be careful not to brown anything.
2 Add the salmon and the clams. After a minute add the wine and fish stock; leave to steam for a minute; then add the parsley and the mustard, mixing well. Season with salt and pepper.
3 Turn the salmon over, cover the pan with a closely fitting lid and cook until the clams are fully open. Sprinkle with paprika, if using, and serve with crusty bread.

Salmon stuffed peppers

I cannot overemphasise how wonderful these peppers are, with their creamy filling and cheesy topping. This works equally well with red or green peppers, and looks best when the peppers can stand up on their own.

SERVES 6
250–300g salmon fillet, cooked
6 red or green peppers
100g fresh breadcrumbs
250–300ml double cream
handful of finely chopped parsley
salt and pepper
1 tbsp butter
50g Cheddar cheese, grated

1 Preheat the oven to 180°C/gas mark 4.
2 Flake the salmon, removing the skin and checking for bones.
3 Slice off the tops of the peppers and set aside. Cut out the centres of the peppers, scraping out the seeds. Very finely chop the edible parts of the pepper 'lids' and mix with the breadcrumbs, cream and parsley. Season to taste. Add the salmon and mix gently.
4 Use the mixture to stuff the peppers, then place them in a roasting pan and pour in a little water.
5 Divide the butter into six pieces and place one piece on top of each stuffed pepper, then add the grated cheese. Bake for 30 minutes or until the tops are browned.

Warm salmon and rocket salad

The lemony vinaigrette makes this a delicious way to serve salmon. I sometimes find the flavour of rocket a little harsh, and you can use other leaves if you prefer, such as young spinach and beet leaves, or a try a combination of rocket, parsley and mint for a change.

SERVES 2

2 salmon fillets, about 100g each
1 tbsp olive oil
50g whole green beans, frozen or fresh
2 large handfuls of rocket leaves

Lemon and garlic vinaigrette

2 tbsp olive oil
3 tbsp lemon juice
1 tsp finely grated lemon zest
1 garlic clove, grated or minced
½ tsp golden caster sugar
pinch of salt
½ tsp dried parsley or 1 tsp finely chopped fresh parsley

1 Preheat the oven to 180°C/gas mark 4, or preheat the grill. Brush the fish with the oil and grill or bake until just cooked. Leave to one side, keeping it warm.
2 Steam or microwave the beans for 3–4 minutes until tender. Drain well and leave to one side.
3 Put all the vinaigrette ingredients into a jar or bowl and shake or whisk until well combined.
4 Place the rocket leaves in a serving bowl. Flake the fish and place in the bowl with the rocket. Stir in the beans.
5 Drizzle over the vinaigrette and toss everything together gently. Serve immediately.

Salmon and asparagus parcels

These are a special treat for a dinner party or a Sunday lunch. The recipe calls for puff pastry, and although I like making my own, ready-made puff pastry really is very good, maybe lacking a little soul but considerably less rustic.

SERVES 4
500g puff pastry
4 salmon fillets, about 180g each
80g butter, softened
1 tbsp chopped chives
salt and pepper
pinch of grated nutmeg
8 asparagus spears
1 small egg, beaten with 1 tbsp milk

1 Preheat the oven to 200°C/gas mark 6. Oil a large baking sheet.
2 Cut the pastry into eight equal portions and roll them out into rectangles measuring about 23 x 15cm. Place four of them on the baking sheet.
3 Place a salmon fillet in the centre of each pastry rectangle.
4 Beat the butter with the chives, salt, pepper and nutmeg. Spread an equal amount of the butter on top of each fillet.
5 Trim the asparagus to fit the fish and lay two asparagus spears on top of each fillet.
6 Brush the edges of the pastry with a little of the beaten egg and lay the second piece of pastry on top. Press down to seal then pinch the edges with your finger and thumb all the way round the parcels. Brush with the rest of the egg. Using a sharp knife, make three slashes across each parcel.
7 Bake the parcels for 25–30 minutes or until the pastry has risen and is golden brown. Serve with mixed green vegetables, such as green beans, broccoli and spring greens, and a few buttered boiled new potatoes if you wish.

Salmon fish cakes

I adore fish cakes, with their crisp coating and soft tasty centre.
Make your breadcrumbs in the morning and leave to dry in
the air for an hour or two; this give the coating a crispy finish.

MAKES 6
380g salmon fillets
450g mashed potato
1 tsp English mustard
2 tbsp chopped fresh parsley or dill
2 tbsp single cream
salt and pepper
3 rounded tbsp plain flour, plus extra for dusting
1 egg, beaten
150g homemade breadcrumbs (see above)
oil for frying

1   Steam or poach the salmon for about 5 minutes until the fish is
    cooked. Drain off all juices and flake into a bowl.
2   Mix the mashed potato with the mustard, herbs, cream and salt and
    pepper to taste.
3   Combine the fish with the potato, but don't overmix: keep chunks of
    fish for flavour and texture.
4   Dust your hands with flour, then form the mixture into six equal
    balls. Press down lightly to form patties.
5   Put the flour, egg and breadcrumbs into three bowls.
6   Heat sufficient oil in a frying pan to come a third of the way up the
    fish cakes.
7   Dip the fish cakes first into the flour, then into the egg to coat all
    over, and finally coat them in the breadcrumbs.
8   Place the fish cakes in the hot oil and fry for 3–4 minutes, then turn
    and fry the other side for 3–4 minutes. Serve immediately: they lose
    the crispness if they are kept warm for too long.

Smoked salmon pasta sauce

Probably one of the quickest pasta sauces I make; this is wonderful with tagliatelle. It doesn't have to be salmon, any smoked fish will do, though I tried this with smoked trout and it was a little too strongly flavoured for my liking.

SERVES 2

150g crème fraîche
2 tbsp soft cream cheese
150g sliced smoked salmon, chopped
juice of ½ lemon
1 tbsp chopped fresh parsley
black pepper and a pinch of salt
grated Parmesan or Grana Padano cheese to serve

1   Heat the crème fraîche, soft cheese, salmon and lemon juice in a saucepan over a gentle heat, stirring until the cheese has combined with the crème fraîche.
2   Stir in the parsley, pepper and salt to taste. Heat until it bubbles, then serve at once with your favourite pasta and plenty of grated cheese.

Salmon mousse

I sometimes make this wonderful mousse with homemade cream cheese – and you can replace the smoked salmon with homemade gravadlax if you like. It is really easy to make, and must be kept refrigerated before serving.

SERVES 6
400g smoked salmon
200g cream cheese
zest and juice of 1 lemon
handful of chopped fresh dill (optional)
salt and black pepper

1 Set aside 100g of the salmon; chop the rest and add to a food processor.
2 Add the cream cheese, lemon zest and juice and dill and pulse to a creamy mixture. Season to taste. Chill the mousse in the fridge for at least an hour.
3 To serve, spoon on to Melba toast or crackers and neatly fold a piece of the reserved salmon on the top.

Variation
★ For an alternative presentation you can lay the reserved (thinly sliced) smoked salmon on a work surface, slightly overlapping, and pipe the mousse into the centre, then roll up the salmon like a swiss roll. Chill in the fridge for an hour before slicing into individual pieces, using a sharp knife.

Spanish omelette with smoked salmon

I usually make omelettes with a dash of water added to the egg, so that when it hits the hot pan the steam lightens the egg. However, in this case, beating the eggs is more about getting air into the egg mixture to create a bubbly base. Consequently, when grilled, the whole thing rises slightly and is very light.

SERVES 2

2 tbsp light olive oil
250g potatoes, peeled and diced
1 small red onion, finely chopped
6 eggs
black pepper to taste
2 tbsp chopped fresh chives
4 slices smoked salmon, torn into thin strips
2 tbsp grated pecorino cheese

1   Heat the oil in a frying pan, add the potatoes and fry for about 8 minutes or until the potatoes start to brown.
2   Add the onion and fry for another few minutes. The potatoes should be tender in the centre and crispy on the outside.
3   Meanwhile, beat the eggs thoroughly with some black pepper and the chives.
4   Place the salmon over the potato mixture and pour over the eggs. Cook over a medium–low heat so the omelette sets but doesn't burn.
5   Preheat the grill to hot.
6   After about 10 minutes, when the omelette looks set, sprinkle the pecorino over the top and place under the hot grill for a minute or so to brown the top. Serve hot with a green salad or some slices of beef tomato drizzled with balsamic vinegar.

Variation

★ If you prefer your omelette runnier, rather than set under the grill, cook the potatoes and onion in the pan first, then remove them while you cook the eggs. Put the potato and onion mixture, the smoked salmon and grated cheese on half of the omelette and fold it over in the French manner.

Trout

The salmon might be the king of fish, but the trout is the prince. Lithe, clever, great sport and wonderfully tasty, trout is the ideal catch-and-eat fish. Of course, you can buy them too, and they are widely farmed.

There are two species of trout in the UK: the indigenous brown trout and the rainbow trout, originating in the United States. There is a slight difference in flavour; some would say the difference is very noticeable. Most usually caught with a fly (an artificial lure, rather than natural bait), they range in size from 500g in northern Pennine rivers to nearly 2kg in southern English chalk streams. They also change their characteristics according to the water they live in and a trout caught in a deep river will look quite different from one in a fast-flowing moorland stream.

Trout are seldom filleted; they are available prepared this way, but if you want to avoid all the fine bones you'll have to check the fillets. Generally trout are simply gutted and cleaned, and cooked with their heads and skin on. There is more work involved in eating a trout than with most other fish, but who cares? It simply prolongs the wonderful experience. For this reason it is always preferable to serve trout on a piping hot plate.

Fried trout with lemon

This is easy to prepare and a wonderful way to eat trout. Put the pan of cooked trout on something heatproof in the middle of the table, serve with hunks of freshly baked bread and butter, and dig in!

SERVES 2
2 trout, cleaned
salt and pepper
1 lemon
25g butter
1 tbsp light oil

1 Score the trout skin with a sharp knife, partly to increase the penetration of the heat and partly to make it look pretty when cooked. Season inside and out.
2 Cut the lemon into thick slices. Heat the oil and butter in a frying pan and add the lemon slices.
3 Add the trout to the pan and cook for 4 minutes on one side and 3 on the other, basting the fish with the lemony oil. Serve with big chunks of bread and butter.

Grilled trout in leek

This is a classic English way of grilling trout, for which you need good-sized leeks. The leek does impart some aroma, but its main function is to keep the force of the grill from burning the fish.

SERVES 2
2 trout, cleaned
1 lemon, halved
salt and pepper
2 large leeks
1 tbsp butter

1 Rub the inside of each fish with half a lemon, squeezing as much juice into the flesh as you can. Season inside and out. Preheat the grill to hot.
2 Cut each leek lengthways down one side only, so you can open it out to create a wrapping for your trout. Lay each trout on the leek leaves, with plenty of overlap to make a parcel, and spread the top surface of the trout (not the leek) with butter.
3 Tie up the parcels with string and grill for 4 minutes, by which time the butter will have infused the fish.
4 Turn over and grill the other side for 3 minutes. Remove the leek leaves and serve.

Pan-fried trout with almonds, croutons and pancetta

Bacon goes well with trout, as do almonds. For this recipe, I like to use thickly cut lardons of unsmoked pancetta (Italian-style bacon). The lardons are best if they are reasonably small.

SERVES 2
2 trout, cleaned
salt and pepper
2 tbsp butter
light olive oil for frying
100g pancetta lardons
150g bread, cut into 1cm cubes
50g flaked almonds

1   Season the trout inside and out. Heat 1 tablespoon of the butter and
    another of olive oil in a frying pan and fry the trout for 4 minutes on
    each side. Remove the fish from the pan and keep them warm in
    a low oven.
2   Add the remaining butter and the lardons to the pan and cook for
    3–4 minutes until the lardons are golden brown. Add the bread
    cubes and cook until crisp and golden brown. Finally add the flaked
    almonds and toss gently in the hot pan for 1–2 minutes until they
    just begin to turn golden.
3   Serve the trout with the bacon mixture spooned on the top and
    watercress on the side, with a mustard sauce.

Baked trout wrapped in bacon

This is an old recipe, and is particularly wonderful on the barbecue, or even an open fire. It uses trout fillets, which need to be scrupulously boned – perhaps the hardest part of the whole dish. There is usually no need for salt as the bacon is salty enough.

PER PERSON
1 trout fillet, skinned
oil for greasing
4 generous slices of smoked bacon
juice of ½ a lemon
black pepper

1 Run your fingers lightly over the trout from the tail towards the head, carefully pulling out any small bones you find.
2 Lightly oil a large piece of foil; on top, lay three parallel slices of bacon and one lengthways – at 90 degrees to the others. The three pieces of bacon will wrap around the trout.
3 Lay the trout fillet on the lengthways piece of bacon and then draw the three pieces over to wrap the fish.
4 Sprinkle with lemon juice and season with a little black pepper.
5 There are various ways to cook this:

★ You can wrap the whole thing in the foil and bake at 180°C/gas mark 4 for 25 minutes.
★ You can draw the sides of the foil up like a boat, leaving the top open, and bake or grill for 25 minutes. This will collect the juices, which can be poured over the fish when serving.
★ You can wrap in foil and barbecue the fish, or you can simply place it on the embers of a fire.

Herb butter trout

Fish have been cooked with herbs for at least 2000 years, probably much longer. One method, dating to around AD 770, describes trout and herbs wrapped in burdock leaves and placed in the embers of a fire, where the fish would steam in the herb juices. All the herbs are fresh; if you can't get one or two of them, don't worry.

SERVES 4

125g butter, roughly cubed
10g rosemary leaves, finely chopped
15g mint leaves, finely chopped
handful of parsley, finely chopped
handful of fennel leaves, finely chopped
handful of chives, finely chopped
5g thyme leaves, finely chopped
salt and pepper
4 trout, cleaned

1   Put the butter into a bowl and warm slightly. Mix all the herbs together and then add to the butter and stir well. Don't use a blender as you will lose juice. Season to taste.
2   Use the herb butter to stuff the cavity of each fish. Place in a baking dish and leave in the fridge for a few hours to infuse the flesh with the herb flavours.
3   Remove from the fridge for an hour before cooking.
4   Preheat the oven to 180°C/gas mark 4.
5   Bake for 30 minutes, occasionally basting the fish with the juices. Serve with buttered boiled potatoes.

Trout with parsley and lime butter

When you eat this you will see how wonderful simple cooking can be. Trout, butter, salt and pepper, parsley and lime. That's it!

SERVES 2
4 trout fillets, pin-boned
150g butter
salt and pepper
50g fresh parsley, finely chopped
juice of 1 lime

1 Run your fingers lightly over the trout fillets from the tail towards the head, carefully pulling out any small bones you find.
2 Melt the butter over a low heat. Remove from the heat. Preheat the grill to moderate.
3 Lay the trout fillets skin down on a grill. Brush the surface with some of the melted butter and season liberally with salt and pepper.
4 Grill for 5–7 minutes. You will not be turning this fish over, so the cooking time will depend on the thickness of the fillet.
5 Return the butter to the heat and beat in the parsley and lime juice. Serve the fish with the sauce drizzled over.

Eastern marinated trout

Our family likes all things Chinese, and this sweet marinade of soy sauce, garlic and honey really enhances the flavour of trout.

SERVES 4–6
4–6 trout fillets
2 tbsp groundnut oil
2 shallots, finely chopped
3–4 garlic cloves, grated
150ml soy sauce
3 tbsp honey
few dashes of sesame oil

1 Make sure the trout is descaled, and check that all the tiny bones are removed, then score the skin with a sharp knife.
2 Heat a little of the oil in a pan and cook the shallots and garlic until softened but not browned. Add the soy sauce and honey, bring to the boil and stir until the honey has dissolved. Pour the marinade into a glass jug or bowl and leave to cool.
3 Put the trout in a dish and spoon the cold marinade over the fish. Cover and leave in the fridge for an hour.
4 When you are ready to cook, heat a little more oil in a frying pan and fry the fish skin down for 4 minutes, adding a few dashes of sesame oil for extra flavour.
5 Turn the fish over and then spoon the marinade over the skin side of the fish, basting as it cooks for 3 more minutes. Serve hot, with rice.

Trout in butter sauce and garlic

This is a brilliant sauce for trout, in fact it is difficult to know which is the star of this show, the trout or the sauce. You can use as much garlic as you like – or none at all if you prefer. This recipe works well with almost any fish.

SERVES 2
2 large trout, at least 600g each, cleaned and descaled
salt and pepper
2 garlic cloves per fish, more (or less) if you prefer, thinly sliced
olive oil for drizzling

Butter sauce
2 shallots, finely sliced
150ml dry white wine
juice of 1 lemon
150g butter
small handful of parsley, finely chopped

1 Preheat the oven to 180°C/gas mark 4. Wash the trout and pat dry. Season inside and out.
2 Lay half of the garlic slices on a large sheet of foil or baking parchment. Place the trout on the garlic, and place the rest of the garlic on top. Drizzle with a little olive oil and close the foil or parchment tightly around the fish. Bake for 25–30 minutes or until cooked completely.
3 To make the sauce, put the shallots, wine and lemon juice into a saucepan with a little of the butter and keep the mixture moving over a medium heat until the liquid has reduced to a third.
4 Add the rest of the butter in small chunks, whisking all the time until it is all incorporated and smooth. Add the parsley and season to taste. Serve the fish smothered in sauce.

CHAPTER 6

Preserved fish

Preserving fish – by salting, drying, smoking, pickling or fermenting – was essential in the days before refrigeration, and throughout the world there are hundreds of local variations on these ancient methods. World travel has led to an exciting interchange of cultures and these days we have access to so many different foods that our grandparents would not recognise half of what we eat.

Smoking techniques are now more controllable and pickling embraces a range of flavourings. The principle of pickling is that salt starts the preserving process and this is maintained by the use of an acidic pickle, usually vinegar, flavoured with sugar and spices. Onion is a common flavouring, perhaps because the onion grows well in the colder climates of northern Europe and Scandinavia, where pickling remains hugely popular.

I've also included some recipes for potted fish and quick pâtés – a simple technique that gives a short preservation time.

Freezing fish
Today, this is probably the most common preservation method for all kinds of fish. Speed, cleanliness and thoroughness are important. Make sure your freezer is working well; this is most important for fish of any kind, which should be stored at -17°C.

First of all you should descale and clean the fish, removing the guts and all traces of blood. Clean thoroughly inside and out with cold water and carefully pat dry. If you like, you can fillet the fish and freeze as fillets. If possible, it is best to vacuum seal the fish before freezing. To defrost fish, transfer it to the fridge to keep it cool while it thaws.

How to sterilise jars
Preserved food often needs to be stored in sterilised jars. If you are a jam-maker you will have your own method of sterilising. I use sterilising tablets for convenience. Alternatively you can put the jars in a low oven (100°C) for 20 minutes and boil the lids for 5–10 minutes.

Salt cod

This is a moist salt cod, not the dry board-like sheets you may have seen hanging up in Italian and Caribbean food shops, but it can be used in most recipes calling for salt cod. This recipe will work well with any meaty fish, such as salmon, pollack or hake. The fish should first be filleted into largish portions (approx. 250–400g), but leave the skin on.

For this recipe you need a non-metallic, non-plastic container, such as a large glass bowl or ceramic pot – preferably something with a lid.

1 Rub a tablespoon of brown sugar into the flesh side of each fillet.
2 Put a layer of salt – Kosher salt or sea salt, not curing salt – in the bottom of the container, then lay the fillets skin down on the salt.
3 Cover with salt, making sure all the nooks and crannies are filled. Then repeat with more fish, finishing with a layer of salt on top.
4 Cover the container and leave in the fridge for a week, by which time the fish should have lost water that will have dissolved the salt. If the topmost fish is not submerged, add a little water to cover it and weigh the fish down with a plate.
5 Leave for a month – or more. It will keep for 3–6 months.
6 Before use, soak in cold water for 24 hours, changing the water several times. You can slice the fish thinly and eat it raw, or use in many different recipes.

Salting anchovies and sardines

Why bother to do this yourself when you can buy them in a tin for little money? Well actually the money is the reason for doing it. A kilo of canned anchovies will cost you £20–50, and you can make your own for about a fiver. It is particularly cost effective with sardines, which in reality are not much removed from large anchovies. It is a simple, if long-winded, process of layering salt and fish.

1kg (at least) anchovies or sardines
sea salt
olive oil

1   Gut, behead and clean out the fish under cold running water, then pat dry. If you are using sardines the fish must be very thoroughly descaled and filleted, removing as many bones as possible.
2   Put a layer of sea salt in the bottom of a glass or ceramic container. For sardines you may want to use a square container and allow space at the top because they need to be weighed down. You get more liquid from these larger fish.
3   Place a layer of fish on the salt, then add more salt, pressing them down as much as possible, then another layer of fish and so on, ending with a layer of salt.
4   If using anchovies, cover them with cling film and leave in the fridge for 48 hours. After this time, you will have some liquor in the bottom of the dish, and you should top this up with brine (dissolve 350g salt in 1 litre of water) to cover the fish. Cover and leave in the fridge for 4 weeks.
5   If using sardines, press down to pack the fish and place a piece of wood or plastic on top of the salt, with a smallish weight on top. Cover and keep in the fridge for 4 weeks.

6 After a month, remove the fish, give them a quick rinse in cold water to remove any excess salt and check for saltiness. If they are too salty, try soaking them in water for an hour and then retest. Repeat until they are how you like them.

7 Pat dry and transfer the fish to sterilised jars. Fill the jars with olive oil, patting the jars to make sure there are no air bubbles in the oil.

8 These will keep for ages in a cool place. Once opened they should be kept in the fridge and eaten within a week.

Hot smoked fish

This works well for oily fish such as mackerel, herring, salmon and trout. They exude oils in the heat of the chamber and the smoky flavour clings to the fish.

It's really easy to do: all you need is a metallic container with a very closely fitting lid and a grill rack inside, and some wood chips. You can use a biscuit tin, or buy a hot smoker, or use a fish kettle. It seems to me that people have fish kettles for two reasons: for showing off their pans in the kitchen – how often do you poach a large salmon? – or for smoking fish. However, once used for smoking it is impossible to keep them pristine. My fish kettle is not really worth looking at, it's all burned!

You can buy wood chips from large supermarkets, DIY stores or garden centres – anywhere that sells barbecue equipment. The best wood for smoking fish is apple wood, which is mild and not overpowering. Never use resinous woods, unless you like pine disinfectant fish!

1   To hot smoke fish, put the wood chippings or briquettes into the bottom of your smoker, place the rack over them and place your smoker on a gentle heat source, such as the barbecue, or the edge of an open fire. It is best to get the smoke going before you add the fish or else the fish will cook before it gets much smoke flavour. When the wood chips start to smoulder, put the fish on the grill rack and put the lid on. As the cooking chamber gets hot, the fish is cooked and smoked at the same time. On average it takes about an hour to hot smoke fish such as herring or trout.

2   You really are best hot smoking outside. If you have a lidded barbecue you can use that for hot smoking directly. My custom-made hot smoking box has a sliding lid, so closely fitting that you can use it in the kitchen – which I have done, with the windows and door open – but it is still a little hit and miss about how much smoke gets out of the smoker.

3 The fish cooks as it smokes, and will last for about a week in the fridge. However, if you first marinate the fish in a brine of 300g salt dissolved in 1 litre of water for about 6 hours it will last a few days longer. Also, if you keep the fish in a vacuum-sealed plastic bag, then it will last a couple of days longer and won't smell the fridge out.

Pickled herring

This is a particularly easy way to pickle herring. Don't worry about stray bones, as they will usually dissolve away in the acidic pickle, and the thinner the fillet the more effective this process becomes.

500g herring fillets
100g sea salt
1.25 litres water
500ml white vinegar or white wine vinegar
60g white granulated sugar
1 tbsp mustard seeds
1 tsp ground allspice
2 tbsp black peppercorns
3 cloves
1 lemon, thinly sliced
1 red onion, sliced into rings

1 Make sure the herring fillets are thoroughly cleaned and all the scales removed (scrape them off with a spoon under running water).
2 Dissolve the salt in a litre of the water and pour into a lidded container. Add the herring fillets and leave in the fridge for 24 hours.
3 Put 250ml water and the vinegar into a saucepan, add the sugar and spices and bring to the boil, simmer for 10 minutes, then leave to cool completely.
4 Put the herring fillets into sterilised jars, add a couple of lemon slices and a generous amount of onion. Pour the cold pickling liquid into the jars and then add the spices left behind, distributing them equally among the jars.
5 Seal the jars and store in the fridge. Unopened, they will last up to 5 weeks.

Variations

★ Add dill seeds and/or a few pieces of star anise to the pickling liquid.

★ To make rollmops, add some chopped gherkin, ginger and celery to the pickling liquid. Lay the herring fillets skin side down and spoon the solid pieces from the liquid on to the fillets, then roll them up and secure each roll with a wooden cocktail stick before placing in sterilised jars.

Pickled white fish

This is an easy way to pickle white fish fillets, and it is really tasty too. The flavour comes from the second cure. You can buy pickling spice, or make your own. You will need a large screw top container or preserving jar.

  1kg white fish fillets, such as cod, pollack, monkfish
  lots of sea salt
  2.5 litres white vinegar
  2 tbsp pickling spice
  1kg white sugar
  2 large onions, sliced into rings
  1 lemon, sliced thinly

  Pickling spice
  2 tbsp mustard seeds
  1 tbsp whole allspice
  2 tsp coriander seeds
  2 whole cloves
  1 tsp ground ginger
  1 tsp dried chilli flakes
  1 bay leaf, crumbled

1 Cut the fish into bite-sized pieces and put into a 3 litre jar in layers, alternating with the salt. Be liberal with the salt. Seal the jar and leave in the fridge for 5 days.
2 Check every other day to make sure the fish is covered with salty brine, pushing it down if necessary.
3 To make the pickling spice, simply mix everything together. You won't need all of it for this recipe, so store in an airtight container.
4 Remove the fish from the jar and wash off all the salt under cold water. Pat dry and leave in the fridge while you make the pickling liquid.

5 Put the vinegar in a pan, add the pickling spice and sugar and bring to the boil until the sugar has dissolved. Leave to cool completely.

6 Sterilise the jar. Add the fish, onions and lemon slices in layers and pour in the cold pickling liquid.

7 Seal and store in the fridge for at least a week before eating. Unopened, this will keep for a couple of months.

Pickled cockles

Do you remember the fish stalls at the seaside? The smells! Ooh, I loved the smells, but it was 30 years before I actually tried the wondrous delicacies. Pickled cockles are easy to make, and eaten in this way they are superb.

1kg cockles in shells, well washed
1 onion, sliced into thin rings
1 litre good malt vinegar
25g brown sugar
15g kosher salt

1 Sterilise a large jar – a kilner jar or some such.
2 Add a little water to a large pan and bring to the boil. Add the cockles, cover the pan with a lid and cook for about a minute over a high heat.
3 Pick the cockles out of their shells and wash them in cold water – there is always a bit of sand in them.
4 Layer the jar with cockles and onion rings, ending with onion.
5 Put the vinegar into a large jug, add the sugar and salt and stir until dissolved, then pour over the cockles. Seal and store in the fridge for at least 24 hours before eating. Unopened, they will keep for up to 14 days.

Variations
★ You can use lemon juice instead of vinegar, adding some sliced lemon to the jar.
★ You can also use white vinegar, but if you are using apple cider vinegar or white wine vinegar, make sure the acetic acid content is at least 5 per cent.

Pickled whelks

When I was a boy I never liked pickled whelks, for a really
stupid reason: they looked like inner ears, laid on a vinegary
tray with onions and green stuff on the fishmonger's shelf.
But if you slice them beforehand, you'd hardly know what
they were. Funny how simple answers to life's problems come
years after the event.

This recipe calls for raw whelks: you can buy them out of
the shell from good fishmongers.

35g sea salt
150ml water
200ml white vinegar
½ tsp mustard seeds
2 cloves
1 tsp black peppercorns
300g whelk meat
1 onion, sliced into rings
large handful of dill, chopped

1   Put the salt, water, vinegar, mustard seeds, cloves and peppercorns
    in a pan and bring to the boil, then leave to cool.
2   Slice the whelks into bite-sized pieces. Put them in a pan, cover with
    water and bring to the boil; boil for a couple of minutes then leave
    the whelks to cool in the liquid.
3   Drain the whelks, discarding the water, and put them in a sterilised
    jar with the onion rings and dill.
4   Pour in the pickling liquid and leave in the fridge for a couple of days
    before nibbling away. Unopened, they will keep for up to 10 days.

Quick mackerel pâté

This is the quickest of all the potted recipes, especially if you use a food processor.

SERVES 4 GENEROUSLY
4 smoked mackerel fillets
300g cream cheese (light or full fat)
2 tbsp natural yogurt
juice of 1 lemon
1 tsp horseradish sauce
black pepper

1 Remove the skin from the fish and place the fillets in a food processor. Add all the other ingredients and pulse until evenly combined. Alternatively, place all the ingredients in a bowl and mash together with a large fork.
2 Spoon the mixture into a serving dish or individual ramekin dishes, cover and chill for 1–2 hours before serving.
3 Store in the fridge, covered, for up to 3 days.

Variation
★ For trout pâté, simply replace the smoked mackerel with (carefully boned) cooked trout fillets. Season to taste with salt and black pepper.

Potted shrimps

The Lancashire coast is famous for its seafood, and especially its shrimps. Potted shrimps make a simple yet tasty starter or quick lunch dish. Add more or less cayenne pepper to taste.

SERVES 2
250g brown shrimp or small cooked peeled prawns
salt and black pepper
80g butter
¼ tsp cayenne pepper

1   Force as many shrimp as will fit into two ramekin dishes and season with salt and pepper.
2   Melt the butter in a small saucepan, add the cayenne pepper and stir to mix thoroughly. Pour the butter over the shrimp and leave to set.
3   Store in the fridge for up to 7 days. Serve with hot toast; the butter from the shrimp will melt into your toast. Delicious!

Tip
★ It's easy to transform a piece of poached or fried hake into something special by adding a spoonful of potted shrimps on top of the freshly cooked fish.

Potted salmon

This makes an excellent first course or sandwich filler.

SERVES 4
200g salmon fillets
50g butter, softened
2 tbsp double cream
a little grated nutmeg
salt and black pepper

1　Steam, oven bake or microwave the salmon until just cooked. Remove any skin and leave to cool in a bowl.
2　Flake the fish and add the butter, cream, nutmeg and salt and pepper to taste.
3　Spoon into four ramekins and place a disc of greaseproof paper on top if storing for longer than a few hours. Chill before serving. Store in the fridge for up to 2 days.

Variation
★ Add a couple of teaspoons of chopped dill or parsley to the mixture if you like.

Gravadlax

The word gravadlax can be translated as *buried salmon*, or *salmon's grave*. Essentially it is cured – not smoked – salmon and is traditionally served sliced thinly and displayed on a platter, accompanied by black bread or rye bread, and a dill and mustard sauce.

It is best if the fillet comes from the centre of the side of salmon, so you have a uniform thickness. Make sure that all the bones are removed before you start. To keep the fish from breaking, leave the skin on the salmon fillet. When you are ready to serve, just slice down to the skin then lift off the slices, leaving the skin behind.

You will need a lidded plastic container to cure the fish. Make sure the container is a tight fit for the fish, so that the cure stays in contact with the flesh.

SERVES 4

approx. 500g salmon fillet (in one piece)
40g sea salt, plus a little extra for the bottom layer
40g light brown sugar
zest and juice of 1 lemon
1 tsp crushed black pepper
handful of dill, chopped
handful of parsley, chopped
25ml white wine or water
25ml white wine vinegar

1   Run your fingers over the salmon fillet to check that all the bones have been removed.
2   Put the salt, sugar and all the remaining ingredients in a blender and whiz to make a paste.
3   Sprinkle a layer of salt in the curing container and place the fish on top. Smear the cure paste over the fish, covering all sides. Close the

container and leave in the fridge for 4 days.

4 To serve, remove the fish and rinse under cold water. Slice thinly and serve with salad or rye bread. It is also lovely with salmon mousse spooned on to the slices and wrapped with the fish.

Fermented salmon

I found this recipe on the internet, and I have tweaked it over the years to make a really tasty bite. It will keep for about two weeks, but it usually vanishes in only a few hours. Perhaps we have salmon fairies!

Although the salmon is cut into chunks, you want thick pieces from the centre of the fish, not the thin tail end.

The idea of using juice from preserved lemons (which are easy to make at home) is to inoculate the fish with healthy fermenting bacteria – a bit like sauerkraut. If you haven't got preserved lemons, simply use lemon juice.

SERVES 4
approx. 500g salmon fillet
100ml water
100ml white vinegar
50ml juice from preserved lemons (or 50ml lemon juice)
25g sea salt
20g sugar
zest and flesh of 1 lemon, finely chopped
large handful of dill, finely chopped
1 tsp crushed black peppercorns

1   Run your fingers over the fillet to check that all the bones have been removed.
2   Put the water and vinegar into a pan with the lemon juice, salt and sugar. Heat gently until the sugar has dissolved, remove from the heat and leave to cool completely.
3   Cut the salmon into bite-sized pieces and randomly stuff into a large sterilised preserving jar with the lemon zest and flesh, dill and peppercorns.
4   Cover the fish with the cool brine and tap the jar to make sure there are no air bubbles. Make sure the fish is covered.

5   Keep at room temperature for a day, then pop into the fridge. Give it at least a week to ferment before consuming with salad or black bread. Unopened, it will keep for up to 2 weeks in the fridge.

Tuyo

This idea comes from the Philippines; it's salted and dried fish, and I usually make it with sardines.

1 First, gut the fish and remove the head, gills and backbone, opening the fish out.
2 Wash the fish in cold water, then soak it overnight in a brine made from 250g salt dissolved in 2 litres of water.
3 Remove from the brine and wash again in cold water. Dry thoroughly.
4 Cover the fish liberally with salt, rubbing it in well, and then leave it on a rack or hook in a cool dry place. It will take about 5 days to dry.
5 Once dry, remove the excess salt under cold running water and pat dry thoroughly once again. Store in jars: the fish will keep for around a month in a cool place.
6 To serve, soak in water for a few hours, then you can serve the fish in a sauce, or with rice and salad, or cooked with peas and rice like a kedgeree.

Variation
★ You can pickle the tuyo in sterilised jars. Mix 250ml olive oil and 250ml vinegar and pour over the fish to cover. Add herbs or spices if you wish: try dill, star anise, or a red chilli.

Mojama (Salted tuna)

This is a Spanish method of drying tuna which rather resembles making a ham. The traditional method calls for a particular triangular muscle along the back of the fish, but you can use any cut you like.

You will need to hang the fish, wrapped in sterile muslin or cheesecloth sheets, in a dark, cool, well ventilated place for about a month.

approx. 1kg fresh tuna fillet
lots of sea salt

1   Wash and dry the fish, then weigh it and keep a note of the weight.
2   Take a ceramic container just large enough to hold the fish, and put a layer of salt in the base.
3   Rub salt all over the fish, liberally covering all the flesh. Place on the bed of salt and cover the dish. Place in the fridge for 24 hours.
4   After 24 hours, remove the fish and discard all the wet salt and liquid drawn from the fish. Feel the fish: it should be firm to the touch. If not, repeat the salting for another 12 hours.
5   Dry the fish thoroughly and wrap in several layers of sterile muslin to keep the flies away, then hang in a dark, cool place for a month. The fish is ready to eat when it has lost about 30 per cent of its original weight. Serve in thin slices.

Note
★ Any bad odours mean the fish is not safe to eat.

Tinned tuna

OK, it's not actually tinned, but preserved in glass jars, which predates the invention of canning. This is a big operation if you do it in the traditional way. The original recipes call for a whole tuna, head and all, and this is by far the best way to cook it if you can manage it. Cooking it with the head spreads oils and gelatine in the meat and adds to the flavour. Obviously you need a very large pot and it is advisable to do this outside, because for most of the process it smells like cooking cat food: your neighbours may not appreciate it! Essentially, you are boiling the fish in salt water for about 4 hours. It is possible to make this without the head, using large tuna chunks, but you'll need several kilos of fish. It simply isn't worth trying with small amounts.

1 medium-sized tuna
at least 5 litres of water
at least 175g sea salt
about 3 x 1 litre bottles of olive oil

1 Gut the tuna, removing all traces of blood; rinse well.
2 Make a 3.5 per cent brine (35g salt to every 1 litre of water) in a large pot: it must be large enough to submerge the fish, and have a closely fitting lid. Make enough brine to completely cover the fish and some more for topping up.
3 Put the tuna into the pot with the brine, bring to the boil and keep at a rolling boil for about 4 hours.
4 Prepare about 20 sterilised jars: not too big, as once opened you'll need to use the tuna within a few days.
5 Leave the tuna in the brine until cool enough to handle. Break the flesh into large chunks and place in the sterilised jars. Fill with olive oil and tap each jar to make sure there are no air bubbles.
6 For the next step you will need a wide pan to hold the jars (you can

do this in two or more batches if necessary); place a tea towel in the bottom to stop the jars from rattling about. Attach the lids and place the jars in the large pan. Fill with boiling water to the neck level of the jars and boil for about 1½–2 hours, topping up with more boiling water when needed.

7 Leave to cool and keep for a month before opening the jars. One good tuna will keep you in tuna and mayo sandwiches for six months!

CHAPTER 7

Prawns, shrimp, lobster and crab

There are millions and millions of tonnes of shrimp and prawns in the seas. In terms of biomass they make up more protein than all our meat agriculture by a long chalk! From krill, the tiny microscopic creatures eaten by more or less everything in the sea, to huge prawns around 30cm in length, the basic form of these animals is very successful. If you believe in reincarnation, statistically speaking you are most likely to come back as a shrimp or prawn than anything else!

In the UK we call smaller varieties shrimp and the larger ones prawns. Dublin Bay prawns, or langoustines, are more like small lobsters. All these creatures, along with their larger cousins crabs and lobsters, are classed as crustaceans: they have hard, jointed shells and lots of legs.

In some parts of Britain it is still possible to push a shrimping net along the sand in shallow water to collect shrimps and cook them on the beach. Because they are small, shrimp and prawns don't reduce the temperature when they are tossed into a large pan of salted boiling water, so they are killed in a second and cooked in only a few seconds more. Killing crabs and lobsters humanely requires a different approach, described in chapter 2.

However, you can avoid a lot of preparation by buying these shellfish ready cooked. Prawns are frequently sold ready peeled, either raw or cooked, and they are often sold frozen.

When it comes to cooking shellfish, there are some important things to remember:

★ If using frozen prawns you should completely defrost them before you cook.
★ Watch out for odd smells, they will only get smellier inside you!
★ I personally think that all but the smallest shrimp need their digestive tract removing. The dark line along the back of the animal

contains its latest meals and can be bitter. It is rarely dangerous to eat, but once you know what it is you will want to remove it. Simply slice along the back and tease out the tract, possibly running the creature under the tap afterwards.

★ As a rough guide, shrimp and prawns are just perfectly cooked when they make a 'C' shape. Straight ones are undercooked and those twisted or in rings are overcooked.

★ The Indian Ocean is teeming with prawns; these are warmwater prawns and a lot of them are now farmed. I avoid these, for a number of reasons, including heavy pesticide use, feeding lagoons that use 400kg of chicken poo per hectare to grow algae for the fry to feed on, and the abysmal conditions of some of the processing factories, especially in Cambodia and Vietnam. Choosing organic king prawns is your best option, and I would always prefer to be sure about the provenance.

Prawn pasta salad

This great for a lunch dish, served on a bed of salad leaves, or as part of a buffet, in which case double the quantities.

SERVES 2 AS A LIGHT LUNCH
150g dried wholewheat pasta
150g large cooked prawns
about ½ a cucumber, or less if it is a large one
100g crème fraîche
50g mayonnaise
1 tbsp tomato purée
½ tsp paprika, plus extra to serve
salt and pepper

1 Cook the pasta according to the packet instructions. Rinse in cold water and leave to drain.
2 Place the prawns in a large bowl. Chop the cucumber into smallish pieces and mix with the prawns.
3 In a separate bowl, mix together the crème fraîche, mayonnaise, tomato purée and paprika. Season to taste.
4 Stir the cooked pasta into the prawns and cucumber. Add the crème fraîche mixture, stirring well. Transfer to a serving bowl and sprinkle with a little more paprika.

Prawn and avocado salad

The dressing makes all the difference to the flavour of the two main ingredients.

SERVES 2 AS A MAIN OR 4 AS A STARTER
150g baby salad leaves
200g cooked king prawns or smaller prawns if you prefer
1 large ripe avocado, peeled and cut into small chunks or thinly sliced

Dressing
1 tsp wholegrain mustard
2 tsp clear honey
juice of 1 lemon
2 tbsp extra virgin olive oil
salt and pepper

1 Place the leaves in a bowl and add the prawns and avocado. Toss everything together.
2 Place all the dressing ingredients in a small lidded jar and shake well together. Pour over the salad and toss gently before serving.

Prawn cocktail

Aw, go on, you know you want to! It may not be as popular as it once was – in the 1970s it was considered the height of sophistication – but it's great fun, and if you make your own mayo and tomato ketchup, or add a chive flower garnish, you can make it really special.

SERVES 4

400g large cooked prawns (preferably in their shells)
2 Little Gem lettuce
4 heaped tbsp mayonnaise
4 tbsp tomato ketchup
juice of 1 lemon
½ tsp Tabasco sauce
1 tsp Worcestershire sauce
1 tbsp chopped chives
chive flowers to garnish (optional)

1 Peel the prawns – you could leave four unpeeled to use as a garnish if you like.
2 Wash and trim the lettuce – shred it if you prefer – and use to line four serving glasses.
3 Mix together the mayonnaise, tomato ketchup, lemon juice, Tabasco and Worcestershire sauce.
4 Arrange the prawns on the lettuce and pour over the sauce. Sprinkle with the chives and add a chive flower to each dish if you like.

Prawns with chilli pasta sauce

Raw prawns are best for this recipe. They have a richer flavour than cooked prawns and are less likely to become tough when cooked in the sauce. If you use frozen ones, defrost them before cooking.

SERVES 4

3 tbsp olive oil
1 small onion, chopped
2 garlic cloves, chopped
1–2 red chillies, finely chopped
350g raw prawns
500g carton passata
2 tsp sugar
salt and pepper

1 Heat the oil in a pan, add the onion and garlic and fry gently without browning for a few minutes.
2 Add the chillies, stir well and fry for a minute. Add the prawns and cook until they turn pink.
3 Stir in the passata and sugar and season to taste. Serve with your favourite pasta.

Gamberoni grilled with garlic and white wine

If you are looking for a romantic starter, look no further. Picking at prawns in a sauce, getting all messy, is the perfect start to a *late evening*. This is very much the Italian version, but you can adjust the flavourings: try adding a little lemongrass or perhaps some five spice for an oriental twist.

SERVES 2
25g butter, plus melted butter for brushing the prawns
2 shallots, very finely chopped
2 garlic cloves, crushed and chopped
150ml dry white wine
100ml fish stock
50ml passata
½ lemon, thinly sliced
salt and black pepper
10 raw king prawns in their shells

1   Heat the butter in a frying pan over a medium heat, add the shallots and garlic and cook until translucent.
2   Add the wine, stock, passata and lemon slices, bring to the boil and season to taste. Set aside.
3   Preheat the grill. Brush the prawns with a little melted butter and then grill for about 2–3 minutes on each side. Pour the sauce into two warmed deep plates and serve the prawns on top.

King prawn kebabs

These are best cooked on a barbecue, but can be grilled too.

MAKES 4 LARGE KEBABS
2 tbsp clear honey
1 tbsp soy sauce
juice of 1 lemon
dash of Worcestershire sauce
1 tbsp finely chopped fresh parsley
2 courgettes, cut into 10 equal slices
1 large or 2 smaller red peppers, cut into 10 pieces
20 large raw king prawns, shelled

1 Mix together the honey, soy sauce, lemon juice, Worcestershire sauce and parsley.
2 Thread a slice of courgette or pepper on to each of four skewers. Add a prawn to each skewer. Continue to fill the skewers, alternating pieces of courgette or pepper with the prawns.
3 Place the skewers in a shallow dish and pour over the honey mixture so it coats all the kebabs. Cover and leave in a cool place for 30 minutes.
4 Preheat your barbecue or grill.
5 Cook the kebabs for 4–5 minutes, turning halfway through the cooking time, making sure the prawns are cooked through. Serve hot with salad or on a bed of vegetable rice.

Goan-style prawn curry

Goa, on the coast of southern India, was a colony of Portugal for many years, and has a distinctive cuisine. This is a typical prawn curry that is not too hot.

SERVES 2–4 (DEPENDING ON HOW GREEDY YOU ARE, AND WHETHER YOU ARE SERVING OTHER DISHES)
2 tbsp sunflower or rapeseed oil
1 small onion, finely chopped
3 ripe tomatoes, chopped
350g frozen prawns, defrosted, or raw shelled ones
salt

Curry paste
3 large garlic cloves, grated
2cm piece of fresh ginger, chopped or grated
½–1 tsp dried chilli flakes or a mild red chilli pepper, chopped
1 tsp ground cumin
1 tsp turmeric
½ tbsp mustard seeds
2 tbsp white wine vinegar
2 tbsp tomato purée
1 rounded tsp soft brown sugar
½ tsp ground black pepper
¼ tsp ground cloves
1 tsp garam masala

1 Combine all the curry paste ingredients in a bowl and mix thoroughly.
2 Heat the oil in a frying pan and gently fry the onion and tomatoes until they are very soft. Add a splash of hot water.
3 Stir in the curry paste mixture and bring to a simmer. Simmer for 10 minutes.
4 Add the prawns and simmer for 10 more minutes. Serve with rice or noodles.

Prawns with chicken and rice

This is inspired by paella. We once spent a fortune on a paella in Palma, Majorca. It was served on a platter the size of a dustbin lid and cost about £75 in 1982! We were completely stuffed, and slept through the bus journey to the other side of the island. At the time I thought paella was a seafood recipe, but later I met a Spanish chap selling it in a market. He explained that the dish was originally made from rabbit and game, not seafood at all.

SERVES 4

3 tbsp sunflower or rapeseed oil
1 onion, chopped
3 garlic cloves, chopped
1 red pepper chopped
1 red chilli, chopped
3 boneless chicken thighs, chopped
50g chorizo, diced
250g short-grain rice (paella rice)
pinch of saffron
150ml dry white wine
300ml chicken stock
½ tsp dried thyme
1 tsp paprika
80g frozen or fresh peas
salt and black pepper
250g raw prawns, shelled
6 cooked prawns in their shells
2 tbsp chopped fresh parsley

1 Heat the oil in a large frying pan, wok or paella pan and fry the onion, garlic, red pepper and chilli together until the onion is translucent.

2 Add the chicken and chorizo and cook for 5 minutes or so, stirring constantly.

3 Stir in the rice, then add the saffron, wine and stock and bring to the boil, then simmer for 10 minutes.

4 Stir in the thyme, paprika and peas. Season with salt and pepper to taste and simmer for 2–3 minutes or until the rice is almost cooked.

5 Add the prawns and parsley and simmer for 2–3 minutes. Serve immediately.

Prawn tart

A rich and satisfying dish for lunch.

SERVES 4
350g puff pastry
250g cooked prawns, defrosted if frozen
100g Red Leicester cheese, grated
100g cheddar or Gruyère cheese, grated
4 eggs
200ml single cream
50ml milk
1 tbsp chopped fresh parsley
salt and black pepper

1 Preheat the oven to 190°C/gas mark 5. Grease a 20cm round flan tin.
2 Roll out the pastry fairly thinly and line the flan tin.
3 Lay the prawns evenly over the pastry and scatter the cheese over
   the top.
4 In a bowl or jug, combine the eggs, cream, milk and parsley, then
   pour over the prawns and cheese. Season to taste with black pepper
   and a little salt if you wish.
5 Bake for 30 minutes until the pastry is golden and crisp and the
   filling is just set. Serve hot or cold.

Prawn rolls

This is my take on a combination of Chinese spring rolls and sausage rolls. Delicious and crisp, they're great for picnics and buffets, eaten hot from the oven or cold.

MAKES 20–24

2 tbsp vegetable oil, plus extra for brushing the pastry
2 tsp sesame oil
3–4 spring onions, chopped
1 garlic clove, chopped
1 red pepper, thinly sliced
200g cooked white rice
80g bean sprouts
1 tbsp soy sauce
2–3 tbsp sweet chilli sauce
250g cooked prawns
6 sheets filo pastry

1   Preheat the oven to 200°C/gas mark 6 and grease a large baking sheet.
2   Heat the oils in a wok or frying pan and cook the spring onions, garlic, red pepper and rice together for 2–3 minutes.
3   Stir in the bean sprouts and cook for a further 2 minutes.
4   Stir in the soy sauce and chilli sauce and a splash of hot water. Add the prawns and stir well to coat the prawns in the sauce. Turn off the heat.
5   Lay a sheet of pastry on a work surface and brush with oil. Cover with a second sheet of pastry and again brush with oil. Using a third of the prawn mixture, spoon it in a line down the pastry, off centre, so it is closer to one edge. Roll up tightly from the closest edge and tuck in the free edges at either end.
6   Place the roll on the baking sheet seam side down. Repeat with the remaining pastry sheets. Brush the rolls with more oil and bake for 15–20 minutes. Leave to cool for 10–15 minutes, then cut into 3–4cm lengths using a sharp knife. Serve hot or cold.

Lobster Thermidor

This recipe was created in Paris in the late nineteenth century by the French chef Auguste Escoffier and took its name from a play by Sardou, *Thermidor*, that was very popular at the time. The dish remains popular to this day.

SERVES 2

1 largish lobster, cooked
20g butter
2 small shallots, finely chopped
300ml fish stock
50ml dry white wine
½ tsp Dijon mustard
50g cream cheese
50ml double cream
dash of Tabasco sauce
2 tbsp chopped fresh parsley
squeeze of lemon juice
salt and pepper
40g mature Cheddar or Parmesan, grated

1   Using a sharp, heavy knife, chop the lobster in half lengthways: first chop through the top of the head, between the eyes; then turn the knife round and chop through the shell to split the lobster in half. Pull out and discard the dark intestinal thread that runs the length of the body, the stomach sac just behind the eyes, and the gills. Keep any greenish or brownish paste-like bits: these are deliciously rich-tasting.
2   Remove the meat from the body and place in a bowl. Crack the claws, remove the meat and add to the bowl.
3   Wash the head in cold water and dry well with kitchen paper. Lay the half shells in a shallow roasting pan. Chop up the meat and spoon into the shells.

4 To make the sauce, melt the butter in a pan and gently fry the shallots. Add the stock and wine and bring to the boil, then turn down the heat to a fast simmer and reduce the liquid by half.
5 Add the mustard, cream cheese, cream and Tabasco and stir over a gentle heat until the cheese has melted into the sauce. Add the lemon juice and parsley, stir well and remove the pan from the heat. Season to taste.
6 Preheat the grill. Spoon the sauce mixture over the lobster meat. Sprinkle with the grated cheese and grill for about 3 minutes until golden brown.

Crab toasties

This is a lovely snack, a cheesy crabby oniony mix with mayo spread on pieces of baguette, toasted. For the cheese, I like to use a mix of halloumi, because it doesn't melt, and Brie, because it does. And if you want to sprinkle a little grated cheddar or Gruyère over the mix before you grill it, I'm not going to stop you!

SERVES 6–8
about 12 slices of baguette, sliced diagonally
250g crabmeat
150ml mayonnaise
150g cheese
½ tsp salt
1 red onion, very finely chopped

1 Toast the bread on one side and then remove from the heat.
2 Mix all the other ingredients. Spoon the mixture over the bread and place under the grill for 2–3 minutes. Serve hot.

Dressed crab

The delight of sunny British seaside holidays. Wonderful crabs with their meat prepared and put back in the shells, slices of lemon and buttered brown bread (real brown bread like it used to be, not the pap we get these days).

1 Kill a large crab as described in chapter 2 and cook it in salted boiling water for 20 minutes (around 12 minutes per kilo). Alternatively, buy a ready cooked crab.
2 Twist off the claws and the legs. Crack open the claws by hitting with the back of a heavy knife. Use a skewer to pull out the flesh and set aside. Make sure there are no pieces of shell in with the meat.
3 Turn the crab on to its back. At the bottom of the crab you will see a flap. Using your thumbs, push upwards to remove the underside shell. You will see the greyish, feathery gills, known as dead men's fingers, which should be discarded. Pull out and discard the mouth parts, with the stomach and intestinal tract.
4 Pull out all the white meat, picking it out of the crevices, and the brown meat and keep in separate bowls.
5 Wash out the top shell and leave to dry. You will see a line around the underside of the shell: you can break this piece of shell away to make it easier to fill the shell.
6 Season the crabmeat with a little salt and pepper. Some people add a little vinegar, or some mustard to the brown meat.
7 Line the shell with some Little Gem lettuce leaves – simply for decoration – and then put the meat back in the shell. You can either keep the white and brown meat separate, or mix them. Garnish with parsley.

Chilli crab cakes

I owe this idea to Chef John of FoodWishes.com. He uses
a high proportion of crabmeat, keeping some of it in large
chunks, which could be a recipe for disaster – because your
cakes will want to fall to pieces – but it's oh so tasty.

SERVES 4–6
2 eggs
100g fresh breadcrumbs
2 tbsp sweet chilli sauce
2 tbsp mayonnaise
salt
400g crabmeat – the white meat, plus some claw meat
100g dried breadcrumbs
50g butter

1 In a bowl combine the eggs, fresh breadcrumbs, chilli sauce,
   mayonnaise and a little salt and mix well.
2 Mash up the white crabmeat but leave the claw meat in large chunks
   (about 1cm square). Add all the crabmeat to the breadcrumb mix
   and fold to combine evenly. Chill for about 1 hour.
3 Spread the dried breadcrumbs in a shallow plate. Using your hands,
   shape the crab mixture into small cakes.
4 Heat the butter in a frying pan until gently foaming, add the crab
   cakes and fry for about 4 minutes on each side, turning them
   carefully. Serve with lemon wedges, tartare sauce or more chilli
   sauce.

CHAPTER 8

Squid, mussels, clams and other shellfish

I used to think that because I could never bring myself to eat a snail, I'd have the same problem with their sea-dwelling cousins. Then it dawned on me that I loved cockles and scallops and they, like snails, are molluscs – so what's not to like? That realisation opened my eyes to a new world of wonderful food, as well as to some real disasters. You see, this meat has to be cooked either very quickly – a minute at most – or very slowly, around an hour or more at a very gentle heat.

You may wonder how squid, cuttlefish and octopus fit in to the picture: are they even shellfish? Well, they are officially molluscs, although the 'shells' of squid and cuttlefish are internal and the octopus has no shell at all. They are known as cephalopods, which means 'head-footed', because their heads are joined directly to their 'feet' (arms/tentacles). In cooking, they need to be treated simply, not washed away with lots of flavours. They do make great additions to stews, but my favourite way to cook squid and cuttlefish is fried quickly in butter and served with a squeeze of lemon juice. In the recipes below, I have written 1kg octopus, but it doesn't really matter – you would be hard pushed to get the weight exactly right.

In America and many European countries there is an amazing range of clams, which – like mussels, scallops and oysters – are bivalve molluscs, meaning that they have a hinged shell in two 'halves', one usually flatter than the other. Most clams and razor shell clams live in the sand; oysters generally live on the sea bed; mussels attach themselves to rocks and vegetation; scallops can propel themselves through the water, though they are pretty sedentary. Most can be eaten either raw or cooked. They generally need little preparation, but you need to check that they are alive and their shells are tightly closed before you cook or eat them. These animals are filter feeders and their food is generally microscopic; there's no room in the shells for a huge gut and they usually eject digested particles in a constant flow: in the case of clams, mussels and oysters the whole animal is edible.

Galician octopus

This is a simple dish from Spain which I am told is a man's dish – I don't know why it can't equally be a ladies' dish! I suppose they mean it's hearty. Actually it is little more than boiled octopus with a simple but tasty dressing.

SERVES 4
1 large onion, cut into quarters
4 garlic cloves, crushed
1kg octopus, cleaned
salt and pepper
1 tbsp paprika
splash of olive oil

1 Bring a large pot of water to the boil and add the quartered onion and garlic.
2 Submerge the octopus in the boiling water and cook for an hour at a rolling simmer.
3 Remove the octopus from the water and leave to rest for 10 minutes.
4 Season with salt and pepper and sprinkle with paprika and a splash of olive oil. Cut into bite-sized pieces and arrange on a sharing platter.

Barbecued octopus

You can use baby octopus for this, if you can get them. This recipe couldn't be simpler!

SERVES 8 FOR SHARING
1kg octopus, cleaned
juice of 1 lemon
salt and pepper
olive oil

1 Preheat the barbecue.
2 Plunge the octopus into a pan of boiling water and cook for about 6 minutes.
3 Remove from the water, pat dry and cut into bite-sized pieces.
4 Arrange the pieces on the barbecue and cook for about 6 minutes, turning them frequently to make sure they are cooked all round.
5 Transfer to a large hot bowl, add the lemon juice, season to taste and finally drizzle olive oil over the meat.

Calamari rings

Squid is brilliant – 'nuff said. People who say it is just like rubber bands have had overcooked squid. This is ideal for sharing as a first course with a bowl of garlic mayo – or with a pile of lemon wedges to squeeze over.

SERVES 6
oil for deep frying
500g cleaned squid, cut into 5mm rings
4 tbsp plain flour
salt and pepper
1 egg, beaten

1 Heat the oil to 180°C in a deep fat fryer; test by dropping a cube of bread into the oil – it should immediately sizzle and should brown within a minute.
2 Dust the squid rings in flour seasoned liberally with salt and pepper, then dip in the egg.
3 Lower them into the hot oil and cook for no longer than 2 minutes.
4 Drain on kitchen paper. Serve hot, with lemon wedges or a dip of garlic mayo.

Creamy mussel pasta sauce

The combination of cream and crème fraîche gives a tangy flavour to the sauce.

SERVES 4
2 tbsp olive oil
3 spring onions or shallots, finely chopped
2–3 garlic cloves, chopped
150ml dry white wine
400g shelled mussels or 1kg mussels in shells, washed and cleaned
180ml single cream
4 tbsp crème fraîche
2 tbsp chopped fresh parsley

1 Heat the oil in a saucepan – if you are using mussels in their shells you'll need a large lidded pan – and fry the onion and garlic together gently.
2 Stir in the wine, raise the heat and add the mussels. If using mussels in shells, cover with the lid and cook until they open, which usually takes about 4 minutes.
3 If using shelled mussels, cook for 2–3 minutes. Stir in the cream and crème fraiche and cook gently for 2 minutes, then stir in the parsley.
4 If using mussels in shells, lift them out of the cooking liquor as soon as they open and keep warm in a bowl. Discard any unopened shells. Stir the cream and crème fraîche into the cooking liquor and simmer for a few minutes, then stir in the parsley. Pour the sauce over the mussels.
5 Serve with your favourite pasta.

Mussels with a creamy bacon sauce

This is heavenly: the salty bacon goes so well with the flavour of the mussels. If you wish, you can lighten the sauce by substituting half-fat crème fraîche for the double cream.

SERVES 2

2 tsp butter or 1 tbsp olive oil
½ small red onion, finely chopped
2 garlic cloves, chopped
6 rashers of bacon, chopped
100ml dry white wine
1kg mussels in shells, washed and cleaned
100ml double cream
black pepper
1 tbsp chopped fresh parsley

1 In a large pan, heat the butter or oil and gently fry the onion, garlic and bacon together until the onion is soft.
2 Add the wine and bring to the boil.
3 Add the mussels carefully so as not to break the shells. Put the lid on and cook for about 4 minutes, by which time all the mussels should have opened. Discard any unopened shells.
4 Carefully lift the mussels into two bowls.
5 Stir the cream, black pepper and parsley into the sauce. Pour over the mussels and serve immediately.

Variation

★ To make a classic moules marinière, use a shallot instead of the red onion and omit the bacon and cream.

Spaghetti with clams and cream

This is inspired by something I had in a restaurant years ago. One of the easiest clam dishes to prepare, it is ready in the time it takes for the spaghetti to cook.

SERVES 3–4
1.5kg clams in shells, washed
400g spaghetti
3–4 tbsp olive oil
4 shallots, finely chopped
2 garlic cloves, finely chopped
200ml dry white wine
150ml crème fraîche or double cream
handful of parsley, finely chopped
salt and pepper

1   Discard any clams that will not close when tapped on the table.
2   Bring a large pan of water to the boil, add a little salt and the spaghetti. Fresh spaghetti will take about 8–10 minutes, dried spaghetti can take up to 15 minutes. Time your clam cooking so you have about 8 minutes to finish the pasta.
3   Heat the oil in a large pan over a medium–high heat and cook the shallots with the garlic until they are translucent. Add the clams and the wine and bring to the boil. Keep shaking the pan until all the clams have opened. Discard any unopened ones.
4   Stir in the crème fraîche or cream and the parsley, season to taste, then turn the heat down low.
5   Drain the spaghetti and return it to its pan. Add the clams and sauce and mix well to coat the pasta. Serve immediately.

Garlic clams

Quick, easy, delicious – but perhaps not the thing to eat before going on a date!

SERVES 2–4
1kg small clams in shells, washed
2 tbsp olive oil
8 garlic cloves, finely diced
100ml dry white wine
100ml fish or vegetable stock
25g butter

1 Discard any clams that will not close when tapped on the table.
2 Heat the oil in a large pan over a medium heat and cook the garlic for about a minute. Then add the wine and stock and boil to reduce the liquid by half.
3 Add the clams and the butter, put a lid on the pan and cook for about 3 minutes or until all the clams are open. Discard any that remain closed. Serve immediately, with crusty bread.

Large clams in oyster sauce

This is simplicity itself. You don't need fresh oysters, as it is made with Chinese-style oyster sauce, a thick, brown, sweetish sauce flavoured with a tiny amount of oyster extract.

SERVES 4
1kg large clams in shells, washed
1 tbsp olive oil
1 onion, finely chopped
3 garlic cloves, finely chopped
125ml water
50ml oyster sauce

1   Discard any clams that will not close when tapped on the table.
2   Heat the oil in a large pan over a medium heat, add the onion and garlic and cook until translucent.
3   Add the water and oyster sauce and bring to the boil, stirring frequently.
4   Add the clams, put a lid on the pan and cook until all the clams are open. Discard any that remain closed. Mix to coat the clams in the sauce and serve.

Clam chowder

This is my take on an American favourite. A chowder is a
soup, often made with cream, clams and potatoes, although
there are many variations. It's usually quite rich, so I've tried
not to use too much butter or cheese.

SERVES 4

2 tbsp butter
1 large onion, finely chopped
1 stick of celery, finely chopped
50g plain flour
450ml fish or chicken stock
2 x 280g cans of clams, drained (about 300g clam meat),
    keeping the liquor
400g new potatoes, cut into small cubes
200ml double cream
50g Cheddar cheese, finely grated
salt and pepper

1   Heat the butter in a pan, add the onion and celery and cook until
    translucent.
2   Sprinkle the flour over the vegetables and stir until incorporated.
3   Add the stock, the clam liquor and the potatoes and cook until the
    potatoes are soft.
4   Add the cream and cheese and stir until the cheese has melted into
    the liquid to give a rich soup.
5   Add the clams and simmer gently for 3–4 minutes. Season to taste.
    Serve hot.

Scallops with bacon and cream

I just love scallops! The type most often found around Britain are the large and succulent king scallops; but sometimes all you can get will be the smaller queenies, in which case you'll need two or three per person. Look for diver-caught scallops, which are far less damaging to the environment than dredged ones. They need to be cooked quickly but thoroughly.

SERVES 4 AS A STARTER
4 large scallops
splash of oil for frying
4 slices of streaky bacon, chopped, or 50g unsmoked
   pancetta lardons
1 small onion, finely chopped
2 garlic cloves, finely chopped
100ml fish or vegetable stock
150ml dry white wine
1 tbsp butter
75ml double cream
50g cheese, such as Cheddar or Gruyère, grated

1   Remove the scallops from their shells and set aside. Wash the deep half shells.
2   Heat a little oil in a pan, fry the bacon until it releases its fat, then add the onion and garlic and cook over a low heat until the onion is really soft, but not brown.
3   Add the stock and the wine and bring to the boil.
4   Preheat the grill to hot.
5   In a separate pan, heat the butter and a little oil over a medium–high heat, add the scallops and cook for 1½–2 minutes on each side.
6   While the scallops are cooking, add the cream to the sauce, stirring.
7   Return the scallops to their shells, cover with the sauce and sprinkle with cheese. Cook under a hot grill until melted. Serve hot.

Oysters Rockefeller

Originating in a restaurant in New Orleans, this is a really simple dish but it needs a lot of bowls, and therefore washing up.

SERVES 6 AS A STARTER
100g spinach
50g fresh parsley
50g spring onions, finely chopped
3 garlic cloves, finely chopped
125g fresh breadcrumbs
125g butter, cubed
25ml Pernod
1 tsp Tabasco sauce
24 oysters, opened to half shells
125g grated cheese, such as Cheddar or Gruyère

1 Preheat the oven to 200°C/gas mark 6.
2 Put the spinach, parsley, spring onions and garlic in a food processor. Pulse to chop and mix. Transfer to a mixing bowl.
3 Put the breadcrumbs, butter, Pernod and Tabasco into the food processor and pulse to create a crumbly mixture. Tip the breadcrumb mixture into the spinach mixture and mix to combine evenly.
4 To keep the oysters steady in the oven, traditionally a layer of rock salt is placed on a baking sheet to a depth of 1cm, and the opened oysters placed on top. Add a teaspoon or two of the green mixture to each oyster, and sprinkle grated cheese on top. Bake for 10 minutes. Serve hot.

Lemon oysters

I'm not one for raw oysters, although you can serve this cold sauce on raw oysters if you wish. Make the sauce the day before you want to serve it, so the flavours can blend and develop. I don't use salt because if you can keep the liquor in the oysters you shouldn't need to add salt.

SERVES 2 AS A STARTER
2 green and 2 red peppers, very finely chopped
2 garlic cloves, grated
juice of 4 lemons
handful of parsley, very finely chopped
10 oysters, opened to half shells

1   Put the peppers and garlic into a glass bowl and mix in the lemon juice and parsley. Leave in the fridge overnight to allow the flavours to develop.
2   About 30 minutes before serving, take the mixture out of the fridge to come to room temperature.
3   Preheat the oven to 200°C/gas mark 6.
4   To keep the oysters steady in the oven, traditionally a layer of rock salt is placed on a baking sheet to a depth of 1cm, and the opened oysters placed on top. Cook the oysters in the hot oven for 10 minutes. Spoon the sauce over the oysters and serve immediately.

CHAPTER 9

Mixed fish dishes

These are the recipes that did not fit easily into one of the other chapters, either because they involve more than one fish, or because it really doesn't matter which kind of fish you use. When it comes to ceviche and sushi, far more important than the type of fish is its absolute freshness.

I've included some family favourites, dishes we cook time and again. One of the ingredients we tend to use a lot is frozen seafood mix, usually comprising prawns, squid and mussels. You can magic up a whole restaurant menu of dishes from that!

Seafood lasagne

This makes a delicious change from the meaty version.

SERVES 4
2 tbsp olive oil
1 red onion, finely chopped
2 garlic cloves, chopped
400g canned chopped tomatoes
2 tbsp tomato purée
100ml dry white wine
about 300g white fish fillets
250g frozen seafood mix, defrosted
100g green beans, chopped into pieces
salt and black pepper
12 sheets of fresh or dried lasagne

Sauce and topping
500ml milk
1 rounded tbsp cornflour
1 tsp mustard powder
80g soft cheese
1 tbsp chopped parsley
½ tbsp chopped chives
black pepper
8 slices chorizo
100g Cheddar cheese, grated

1 Preheat the oven to 180°C/gas mark 4.
2 Heat the oil in a saucepan and fry the onions gently with the garlic.
3 Pour in the tomatoes, tomato purée and wine. Bring to the boil, then
   turn the heat down to a simmer, add the fish and cook for about
   5 minutes.

4 Add the seafood and green beans and season to taste. Simmer gently for about 20 minutes.

5 Meanwhile make the sauce. Heat the milk, reserving 3 tablespoons of cold; blend the 3 tablespoons of cold milk with the cornflour and mustard powder to make a paste. As the milk heats up, whisk in the cornflour mixture. Bring to the boil, whisking gently all the time. Turn down the heat and stir in the soft cheese, herbs and black pepper to taste. Simmer for about 2 minutes.

6 Layer the fish mixture and lasagne sheets in a baking dish and top with the sauce. Lay the slices of chorizo on top and sprinkle with the grated cheddar. Bake for about 40 minutes or until the pasta sheets are cooked.

7 Serve with a salad of chopped cucumber, lettuce leaves and a couple of teaspoons of capers. Dress the salad with the juice of 1 lemon whisked with a tablespoon of olive oil.

Quick bouillabaisse

An authentic bouillabaisse needs lots of preparation: this quick version is nevertheless delicious. It tastes even better if you leave it to go completely cold and reheat gently before serving.

SERVES 4
2 tbsp olive oil
1 small onion, finely chopped
2 garlic cloves, chopped
250g frozen seafood mix, defrosted
100ml white wine (optional)
500ml fish or vegetable stock
500g passata
salt and black pepper
1 tsp dried parsley or 1 tbsp chopped fresh parsley
½ tsp cayenne pepper
50g green beans
50g frozen peas

1 Heat the oil gently in a saucepan; add the onion, cook for a few minutes then add the garlic.
2 Stir in the seafood with its defrost liquor. Add the wine, stock and passata. Season with salt and pepper.
3 Stir in the parsley, cayenne pepper, beans and peas and bring to the boil. Turn down the heat and simmer for about 15 minutes.
4 Leave to stand for about 10 minutes, to allow the flavours to develop. Reheat gently if necessary before serving.

Italian-style fish soup

A light, summery soup; fresh basil adds a Mediterranean flavour.

SERVES 4

350g white fish, all bones and skin removed
700ml fish or vegetable stock
100ml red wine
400g canned chopped tomatoes
2 garlic cloves, chopped
about 8 fresh basil leaves, torn
1 tbsp chopped fresh parsley
salt and pepper

1   Poach the fish in a little water until just cooked. Using a slotted spoon, lift the fish out of the liquid, saving the liquid for the soup. Flake the fish and put to one side.

2   Put the stock, wine, tomatoes, garlic and herbs in a saucepan and bring to the boil. Turn down the heat, stir in the fish and the poaching liquid and simmer for about 10 minutes. Season to taste and serve with croutons or crusty bread.

Creamy fish soup

A seriously rich, filling soup – you are sorry when the bowl comes to an end. It's a basis for experimentation: I use whatever I have in the way of onions, shallots or spring onions, and whatever mushrooms I have to hand. Try it with chopped cabbage stirred in: it's a real eye opener!

SERVES 4

1 tbsp butter
1 tbsp olive oil
1 onion, finely chopped
1 stick of celery, chopped
4 mushrooms, sliced
1 garlic clove, chopped
500g white fish such as coley, whiting or pollack, all bones
    and skin removed, then chopped into chunks
700ml vegetable or fish stock
1 tbsp cornflour
100ml milk
300ml double cream
salt and black pepper
1 tbsp chopped fresh parsley
4 queen scallops
sweet paprika to serve

1 Heat the butter and oil in a saucepan, add the onion and celery and
   cook over a medium heat until the onion is soft but not brown.
2 Add the mushrooms and garlic and stir well. Add the fish and stir
   gently to mix. Pour in the stock and simmer for 5 minutes.

3 Mix the cornflour with the milk (I usually shake them together in a lidded jar). Pour the cornflour mixture into the soup and bring to the boil, stirring gently all the time. Turn down the heat, add the cream, season with salt and pepper and stir in the parsley. Remove from the heat and cover with a lid.

4 Fry the scallops in a little olive oil for 2–3 minutes on each side, then slice into 3–4 pieces.

5 Serve the soup in bowls, place the scallop slices on top of the soup and sprinkle with a little paprika just before serving.

Fish curry

My mouth waters just thinking about this spicy fish dish. Use any white fish for this; I tend to choose haddock or hake.

Ideally, make the curry in advance and then reheat it before serving. This always makes any curry taste better: the flavours blend together and it has more zing. When reheating, do it slowly and make sure the curry is piping hot before serving.

SERVES 4
2 tbsp olive oil
1 small onion, sliced
200ml fish or vegetable stock
350ml coconut milk
450g white fish, cut into chunks

Curry base
1 tsp cumin seeds
1 tsp coriander seeds
1 tsp mustard seeds
1 tsp cayenne pepper
4 garlic cloves, chopped
pinch of salt
3 red chillies, deseeded if you prefer, roughly chopped
4 tbsp water
1 tbsp olive oil
2 tbsp lemon juice

1 Make the curry base, either by putting everything in a small grinder or in a pestle and mortar. If you are using a pestle and mortar, put the seeds in first with the cayenne, garlic and salt and pound together, then add the chillies. Pound again until it is a smoothish paste. Stir in the water, oil and lemon juice.

2   Heat the oil in a frying pan, add the onion and fry gently for about 5 minutes until the onion softens.

3   Add the curry base to the onion and cook for 2 minutes.

4   Stir in the stock and coconut milk and bring to the boil. Add the fish, reduce the heat and simmer for about 12–15 minutes or until the fish is cooked. Leave to cool.

5   When you are ready to serve, reheat gently and serve with boiled rice or chapatis.

Seafood and tomato pasta sauce

Quick, easy and delicious. I used to order this – it was called *pasta pescatore* – when we went to our local Italian restaurant in Leeds when we were at college.

SERVES 4

2 tbsp olive oil
1 small onion, finely chopped
1 red pepper, chopped
3 garlic cloves, chopped
150ml dry white wine
2 tbsp tomato purée
400g canned chopped tomatoes
1 tsp paprika
300g frozen seafood mix, defrosted
salt and pepper
2 tbsp chopped fresh parsley, or torn basil leaves

1 Heat the oil in a saucepan and fry the onion, red pepper and garlic together gently for a few minutes until softened, but not browned: the sauce will be bitter if they brown.
2 Stir in the wine, tomato purée, chopped tomatoes and paprika. Bring to the boil, then turn the heat down to a simmer.
3 Stir in the seafood and any of the liquor and season to taste with salt and pepper. Cook at a gentle simmer for 5 minutes then stir in the parsley or basil. Serve with your favourite pasta.

Traditional fish pie

Our local pub makes one of the best fish pies. Here is my
version of the dish. If you like, you can add three hard-boiled
eggs, quartered, to the fish and prawns before adding the
sauce. We prefer it without eggs.

If you don't want to use wine simply add 50ml extra milk
and the juice of half a lemon. The acidity of the wine or lemon
lifts the flavour of the dish.

SERVES 4–6
150ml milk
100ml dry white wine
100ml water or fish stock
300g chunks of white fish, such as cod, coley, whiting, haddock,
    pollack, hake – use one sort or a combination
80g smoked haddock, cut into pieces
30g butter
1 leek, chopped
1 rounded tbsp plain flour
100g frozen peas, defrosted
1 tbsp chopped fresh parsley
salt and pepper
100ml double cream
80g prawns, defrosted if frozen
about 700g mashed potato
60g Cheddar cheese, grated

1   Preheat the oven to 180°C/gas mark 4.
2   Place the milk, wine and water or stock in a pan and add all the fish.
    Bring to a simmer and cook for about 5 minutes. Turn off the heat
    and lift the fish out of the liquor into a bowl; set aside.

3 Heat the butter in a pan and fry the leek gently until tender. Sprinkle over the flour and stir well. Add the fish cooking liquor slowly, stirring constantly until it thickens.

4 Add the peas and cook for 2 minutes. Stir in the parsley and season to taste with salt and pepper. Remove from the heat and stir in the cream.

5 Place the fish and prawns in an ovenproof dish and pour over the sauce. Mix gently so as not to break up the fish.

6 Spoon the mashed potato over the top and flatten the top if you wish: I like peaks that catch the cheese and go crispy. Sprinkle the top with the cheese. Place the dish on a baking sheet and bake for 30–35 minutes or until the top is golden brown. Serve with steamed green beans or broccoli.

Ceviche

There are so many recipes for this dish from Latin America. Essentially it is a raw fish salad; the fish is 'cooked' by the acidity of the lime juice. I've used white fish, but you can also make it from scallops, prawns and other seafood.

The important thing is that you must use the very freshest fish you can find. It is a good idea to find a really good fishmonger and tell him what you are planning.

SERVES 4
400g white fish fillets, skinned
200–250ml freshly squeezed lime juice
1 tsp salt
1 large red onion, finely chopped
4 large tomatoes, skinned, deseeded and finely chopped
3 garlic cloves, finely chopped
1 red pepper, finely chopped
3 jalapeño peppers, deseeded and finely chopped
handful of parsley or coriander, finely chopped

1　Run your fingers lightly over the fish from the tail towards the head and pull out any small bones. Cut the fish into 1–2cm cubes and place in a bowl with the lime juice and salt. Leave to marinate for 20 minutes. (For a raw texture inside, marinate for 15 minutes; for a more thorough marinade, leave for 25–30 minutes; don't leave it longer than that or the fish will break down.)
2　Put the other ingredients into a bowl and leave in the fridge while the fish is marinating.
3　When the fish is ready, spoon it into the vegetable salsa with some of the lime juice. Serve with tortilla.

Sushi

It isn't within the remit of this book to give loads of recipes for sushi – and in any case, sushi is not actually about fish, it's about rice, but people expect raw and cooked fish when they go to a sushi restaurant, so here's an introduction to the world of sushi.

To begin with, you need some equipment: a sushi mat for rolling and a very, very sharp knife. People who make sushi regularly think nothing of paying hundreds of pounds for a good sushi knife.

You can buy sushi rice in most supermarkets these days. Follow the instructions carefully: generally you need to wash the rice at least three times before boiling it. Some recipes call for sauces to be added, sometimes wine, sometimes a stock. You must let the rice cool completely before making sushi.

It is no use buying just any old fish, which usually needs cooking to be sure it is completely safe to eat. Sushi grade fish, super fresh, can be eaten raw; it is sold in Japanese, and some Chinese, supermarkets. You can get sushi grade tuna, salmon, cod and many other fish.

Your knife needs to be sharper than it has ever been; dip it in water as you use it to give a cleaner cut. This is an important part of the process; you are looking for a cut that is as smooth and exact as possible. Should you use a sawing action to cut through the fish it will be rough at the cut surface, affording an opportunity for bacterial growth. Slice your fish thinly and cleanly.

Nori is often used to wrap sushi. It is made from seaweed – the same as laver in the UK – and it comes in paper-like sheets (about 18 x 20cm) with a shiny side and a dull side. Sushi is made with the shiny side out.

Tuna, cucumber and avocado sushi

This is not difficult to prepare once you have everything at hand. The ingredients here are for just one nori roll; you'll probably want to make more. In fact, I usually cook lots of rice and have some left over. It takes a while to get used to this technique, but any mistakes taste just as lovely as the perfect ones!

MAKES 8 PIECES
1 nori sheet
1 cucumber
1 avocado
approx. 50g sushi grade tuna
approx. 50g sushi rice, cooked and cooled

1 Place your sushi mat on the work surface, then put the nori on top, shiny side down.
2 Peel the cucumber and cut about 12 sticks of cucumber, about 10cm long and 3mm square.
3 Peel and stone the avocado and cut sticks of avocado of similar size to the cucumber sticks.
4 Cut the fish to more or less the same size.
5 Lay sushi rice on the nori in a layer about 5mm thick, leaving a 2–3cm border all round the rice.
6 At the top end of the rice, place a piece of fish, and next to it a piece of cucumber. Repeat along the width of the rice. Place pieces of avocado on top of the cucumber.
7 Wet the nori at the lower edge of the rice and cut it away, leaving 1cm to stick the nori to the other end.
8 Roll up from the top end, using the sushi mat and squeezing quite firmly so the roll is tight. The wet end of the nori should stick to the nori at the other end.
9 Using a wet, very sharp knife, cut the roll into 1.5cm slices.

CHAPTER 10

Fish stock and sauces

Fish stock

All kinds of sauces and soups need a good stock: it makes the difference between plain cooking and something special, and the time taken to make it is well spent.

MAKES ABOUT 500ml

300g fish trimmings (skin, heads, bones) and/or shells from prawns, crayfish, lobster or crabs

1 leek, chopped

2 carrots, chopped

1 bay leaf

½ tsp salt

¼ tsp black pepper

150ml dry white wine

2 tbsp roughly chopped parsley

1 tbsp tomato purée (optional)

800ml water

1 Place all the ingredients in a saucepan, cover with a lid and bring to the boil, then turn down the heat and simmer gently for 30 minutes.

2 Strain the liquid through a fine sieve into another saucepan and simmer until the stock has reduced by half.

3 Use straight away or store in a lidded container in the fridge for up to a week. You can also freeze it: ice cube trays are ideal as you can pop out as many cubes of frozen stock as you need. Store in the freezer for up to 3 months.

Basic fish sauce

Fresh fish is delicious served on its own, but having a sauce to pour over it makes it extra special. When you have poached fish you can use the poaching liquid to make a sauce. If you steam, grill or bake your fish on a piece of foil, you can collect the fish juices to add to this sauce.

SERVES 4
400ml warm milk – or stock, wine or water
30g butter
25g plain flour
salt and pepper

1 Put the milk in a pan, together with any juices from cooking the fish, and heat gently over a low heat.
2 Add the butter and sprinkle over the flour. Using a balloon whisk, whisk the flour into the liquid. Season to taste with salt and pepper.
3 Turn up the heat and bring to the boil, whisking continuously, then turn down the heat and simmer for 2 minutes. So long as you keep whisking, the sauce will thicken smoothly without any lumps.

Variations
★ Parsley or dill sauce – stir in 2 tablespoons chopped fresh parsley or dill after the flour has been whisked in. Leave to stand for 3 minutes before pouring into a warmed sauce boat or jug.
★ Cheese sauce – after the sauce has come to the boil, add 1 teaspoon English mustard and 100g grated Cheddar cheese. For an extra kick, stir in a pinch of cayenne pepper just before serving.

Mornay sauce

White fish fillets become a luxurious dish with a coating of
this rich cheese sauce; put the fish into a baking dish, pour
the sauce over the top and bake or grill until the fish is cooked
through.

SERVES 4
300ml milk
2 strips of lemon peel
1 bay leaf
black pepper
30g butter
25g plain flour
½ tsp English mustard
80g mature Cheddar or Gruyère cheese, grated
2 tbsp double cream
salt

1 Heat the milk with the lemon peel, bay leaf and a little black pepper
   until hot but not boiling. Remove from the heat and set aside for
   15 minutes. Remove the lemon peel and bay leaf.
2 Melt the butter in a saucepan over a medium heat and stir in the
   flour, using a wooden spoon and stirring constantly until smooth.
3 Remove from the heat and gradually beat in the warm milk.
4 Replace over a low heat and stir until the mixture begins to simmer;
   continue to cook for a few minutes until thick and smooth.
5 Stir in the mustard, cheese and cream, remove from the heat and
   continue to stir until the cheese has melted. Season to taste: you
   may not need much salt because the cheese is salty.

Hollandaise sauce

There are many ways to make this classic sauce, but it seems to me that some people worry about it too much. The key thing is to get the egg yolks to gradually *absorb* the butter – so keep beating until you have a smooth sauce.

SERVES 4
2 egg yolks
salt and pepper
2 tsp lemon juice
120g butter

1   In a heatproof bowl, beat the egg yolks for about 1 minute, until they thicken. Add a pinch of salt and pepper and the lemon juice and beat together well.
2   Melt the butter in a small saucepan, preferably one with a lip, then turn up the heat until the butter is hot and spitting.
3   Remove from the heat and, holding the pan in your left hand (if you are right-handed) and a balloon whisk in your right hand, pour the hot butter on to the egg yolks, starting with a few drops and whisking all the time. (To prevent the bowl from slipping, put it on a folded tea towel.) As the butter is absorbed you can begin to pour it in a thin stream. The hot butter cooks and thickens the yolks.
4   Taste and add a little more salt or lemon juice if needed.

Easy tartare sauce

Delicious with fried fish or fish cakes.

SERVES 4–6
4 rounded tbsp mayonnaise
2 small gherkins, finely chopped
1 tbsp capers, chopped
½ tsp Dijon mustard
1 tbsp thick natural yogurt

1   Place all the ingredients in a bowl and mix well. Store in the fridge
    for up to 24 hours. Stir before serving.

Variations
★ Omit the yogurt for a less creamy version.
★ Add ½ tsp creamy horseradish sauce for an extra kick.
★ For an extra tang, add a squeeze of lemon juice.

Easy crust toppings

A crisp crust transforms fillets of fish into something special. Press a thick layer of the crust on top of the fish, then grill or roast until the fish is cooked through. Whiz leftover bread in a food processor to make your own breadcrumbs and keep them in a freezer.

EACH RECIPE MAKES ENOUGH TO COVER 2 LARGE FILLETS.

Lemon and parsley

50g fresh breadcrumbs
zest and juice of 1 lemon
1 tbsp chopped fresh parsley
salt and pepper

1 Place all the ingredients in a bowl and mix well.
2 Place your fish fillets in a lightly oiled or buttered baking dish, brush the tops with oil or melted butter and cover with a thick layer of the crust before cooking.

Variation

★ Replace the lemon and parsley with lime and dill.

Chorizo and cheese

50g fresh breadcrumbs
50g Parmesan cheese, grated
juice of ½–1 lemon
6–8 slices of chorizo

1 Mix the breadcrumbs and cheese in a bowl and add lemon juice to moisten slightly.
2 Place your fish fillets in a lightly oiled baking dish, place the chorizo slices on top and cover with the crust. Allow an extra 1–2 minutes of cooking time to make sure the fish is cooked under the chorizo.

Index

THE FISH BOOK